Meaning

Central Problems of Philosophy
Series Editor: John Shand

This series of books presents concise, clear, and rigorous analyses of the core problems that preoccupy philosophers across all approaches to the discipline. Each book encapsulates the essential arguments and debates, providing an authoritative guide to the subject while also introducing original perspectives. This series of books by an international team of authors aims to cover those fundamental topics that, taken together, constitute the full breadth of philosophy.

Published titles

Forthcoming titles

Meaning

David E. Cooper

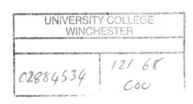
© David E. Cooper, 2003

First published in 2003 by Acumen

Acumen Publishing Limited
15a Lewins Yard
East Street
Chesham
Bucks HP5 1HQ
www.acumenpublishing.co.uk

ISBN: 1-902683-75-7 (hardcover)
ISBN: 1-902683-76-5 (paperback)

British Library Cataloguing-in-Publication Data
A catalogue record for this book is available from
the British Library.

Designed and typeset by Kate Williams, Abergavenny.
Printed and bound by Biddles Ltd., Guildford and King's Lynn.

Contents

1 Preliminaries

This book is both more and less modest in ambition than most English-language philosophical writings on meaning in recent times. In part, this is because the book belongs in a series primarily aimed at students who are no longer beginners in philosophy, so that it has its sights set higher than those of an introductory text-book, but without aspiring to the level of detailed and perhaps technical argumentation expected in a specialist monograph. The main reason for the book's blend of modesty and ambition, however, is different, and owes to the fact that the writings I have in mind have primarily pursued *theoretical* projects in the philosophy of *language*. Let me explain, beginning with the respect in which the book is less modest in ambition than those writings.

Linguistic and non-linguistic

Here are the opening lines of a recent book bearing, like mine, the terse title *Meaning*: "What is meaning? Why are some sounds imbued with it and others not? How, for example, does it come about that the word 'dog' means precisely what it does?" (Horwich 1999: 1). The author takes it for granted that questions about meaning belong to the philosophy of language, and nowhere indicates that anything except words and other linguistic items may have meaning. *The Oxford Companion to Philosophy* entry on meaning follows suit. Questions about meaning, which "present some of the most intractable problems of philosophy", are immediately equated with ones about "linguistic meaning and the way language relates to reality" (Crane 1995: 541). In one respect, the sister entry in *The Cambridge Dictionary of Philosophy* is more generous when it characterizes meaning as "the conventional, common, or standard sense of an expression, construction, or sentence in a given language, *or* of a non-linguistic signal or symbol" (Loar 1995: 471, my italics). In another respect, however, the characterization is narrower, since it excludes such forms of non-conventional linguistic meaning as the poetic and figurative. Moreover, signals and symbols hardly exhaust the range of items that may be spoken of as having meaning. A painting can have meaning without signalling or symbolizing anything. Gardens are not symbols, but on my coffee table is a handsome volume called *The Meaning of Gardens.* Bowler hats are not signals, yet one such hat "returned again and again" in the life of a Milan Kundera character, "each time with a different meaning" (Kundera 1984: 88).

My book is less modest in ambition than most English-language writings in that my concerns are not limited to linguistic meaning, let alone to "conventional" or "standard" linguistic meaning. In spirit, at least, my concerns are closer to those of structuralists, semiologists, hermeneuticists and others whose "preoccupations" are not – *pace The Oxford Companion*'s depiction of "both the 'analytic' and 'continental' traditions" – solely with linguistic meaning. For them, as for me, meaning is not the preserve of the philosophy of language – not, at any rate, unless the term "language" is used in a peculiarly extended way so as to allow for "the language of food", "the language of dress" and the like.

Given our pervasive talk of non-linguistic items having meaning, it is hard to divine the reasons behind a restriction of philosophical concern to linguistic meaning. One generally gets little help from those, like the authors cited earlier, who follow this restriction: it is not one for which they argue, rather one from which they start. I suspect, however, that two different, indeed opposed, trains of thought lie behind the restriction. According to the first, linguistic meaning enjoys a certain centrality. When meaning is assigned to non-linguistic items, this need not be in a different sense of "meaning", exactly; nevertheless, such assignments are derivative from, or depend on analogy with, assignments of meaning to words and sentences. Hence, the real philosophical work must go into explaining linguistic meaning. Those with a taste for it may then proceed, fairly smoothly, to adjust the explanation in extending it to non-linguistic domains.

The difficulty with this train of thought is to identify a relevant sense in which linguistic meaning is "central". Doubtless, the "linguistic turn" taken by analytical philosophy in the twentieth century, with its accompanying conviction that philosophical problems in general may be solved or dissolved by attending to the meanings of crucial terms ("knowledge", "good", or whatever), helped to centre philosophers' attention on the meaning of linguistic items. But not only is that conviction one that many would now want to challenge; it does nothing to show that the meaning possessed by such items is distinctive or peculiarly paradigmatic. It might be granted as well that, in *some* sense, language is "more important" in human life than any other bearers of meaning; but, again, it won't follow from this that the meaning borne by the latter is "secondary" to or "derivative" from the meaning possessed by words. Certainly, there is no good reason to think that linguistic meaning is primary in having "come first". Our ancestors, one suspects, could recognize the significance of one another's gestures and facial expressions, and indeed of natural events, long before they shared a language.

That kind of reply to the first train of thought prompts a second, opposed one. According to this, "meaning" means something quite distinctive when assigned to linguistic items. Scowls can mean anger, clouds can mean imminent rain – but not in a similar, or even analogous, sense to that in which the *words* "scowl" and "cloud" mean something. Nor, the thought continues, is it odd to devote philosophical effort solely to linguistic meaning, for it is this which is "perplexing", "mysterious" and generates seemingly "intractable problems". This is because attributions of non-linguistic meaning can be rendered in a different idiom – "Anger causes scowling", "Clouds are regularly followed by rain", and the like – that is plainly consistent with a "naturalistic", scientific account of the world. Matters are different, however, with statements of linguistic meaning: "'Nuages' means clouds" or "'Les nuages sont noirs' means that the clouds are black" *prima facie* resists rendition in, or reduction to, a purely naturalistic idiom. It's not as if, for example, clouds *cause* the word "nuages". Since what is "perplexing" about meaning, so the thought concludes, is the apparent impossibility of accommodating it within a naturalistic conception, then it is indeed upon linguistic meaning that those specialists in perplexity, philosophers, must focus.

This second train of thought in support of restricting attention to linguistic meaning will fail to persuade someone less sanguine than its followers that the meanings of non-linguistic items can be smoothly and unproblematically rendered in a naturalistic idiom. That marks on maps or in some dance notation give rise to the same "perplexity" as words is not something he will harp on, since he may agree – as his opponents may – that the tools of cartography and dance notation are sufficiently "language-like" for these marks to be credited with linguistic meaning. His point, rather, is that it is hopelessly crude to suppose that talk of meaning in connection with, say, paintings and facial expressions – and even clouds – can be unproblematically eliminated in favour of a naturalistic idiom. (More on this in Chapter 2.)

The train of thought will also fail to impress those who, whatever their stance on non-linguistic meaning, fail to understand why the "perplexity" indicated should be elevated to *the* central, all-consuming problem of meaning. They will, of course, be familiar with the approach of those, like Alfred Tarski (1956) and W. V. Quine (1970), for whom semantic terms, like "meaning", remain "unintelligible" or thoroughly "opaque" unless reduced to or replaced by non-semantic ones congenial to natural science. But they will see this more as a symptom of a scientistic obsession than as providing a reasonable constraint on philosophical enquiry into meaning. At any rate, they will remind us of the many questions about meaning, which philosophers over the centuries have found interesting, that have little or no relationship to a naturalistic programme – questions, for example, about the role of meaning in social explanation or the relevance of an artist's intention to the interpretation of his or her work. And they will remind us, as those examples suggest, that many of those questions concern non-linguistic as much as linguistic meaning.

Here, incidentally, is as good a place as any to insert a warning notice about the phrase "linguistic meaning". As I broadly employ it, it refers to meaning as predicated of linguistic items (words, sentences etc.), uses of them (assertions, questions etc.) and users of them (speakers, writers). (Sometimes, for convenience, I will use "linguistic item" to refer to all of these.) "Linguistic meaning" should *not*, therefore, be construed, on a par with "sentimental meaning" or "figurative meaning", as referring to a *type* of meaning. We should distinguish between the meaning which items of a certain kind have and a type of meaning had by items of, perhaps, different kinds. So we shouldn't be tempted by the phrase "linguistic meaning" into thinking that there must be a distinct type of meaning answering to it.

I am unimpressed, to return to my theme, by the trains of thought lurking behind the restriction to the linguistic of philosophical enquiry into meaning. But what if someone says, "Look, it's language that interests me. I don't have a view on non-linguistic meaning, its relationship or lack of one to linguistic meaning. That's just not my bag, so I'll stick to investigating words and sentences"? As it stands, that is no more objectionable than the restriction of interest self-imposed by someone whose "bag" is the meaning of rituals or of gardens. Horses for courses, after all. There are, however, dangers in such self-denying ordinances.

One is that, by ignoring all but one domain of meaning, someone may be more tempted than otherwise by certain pictures of meaning that should be suspect even in the domain of his particular interest. It is doubtful, for example, that people would have been as attracted as they have been by the so-called "Fido"-Fido conception of a word's meaning – as the object the word names – if they had paid more attention to domains of meaning where this conception is a non-starter: to, for example, ritual and ceremony. ("What object does the Easter procession stand for?" sounds a plainly silly question. "What is the significance or meaning of the procession?" does not.) Again, recent "inferentialist" accounts of sentence meaning (see, e.g. Brandom 1994 and 2000) – in terms, roughly, of rational entitlements to, and commitments made through, assertions – lose their *prima facie* plausibility when attention is paid to the meaning belonging to activities less commonly subjected to rational appraisal than the making of assertions. (To ask about the meaning of a painting would not, typically, involve asking about the artist's entitlement to express what he did.)

A second danger is that someone focused on only one domain may become so fascinated by a feature peculiar to, or especially salient in, this domain that attention is diverted away from the understanding of meaning to a fixation on that feature. A prime illustration is the industry devoted, these days, to the "compositionality" of linguistic meaning – to the fact that the meanings of many sentences are determined by the meanings of their parts. This feature of language has inspired many philosophers, like Donald Davidson (1984), to impose what Paul Horwich calls a "compositionality constraint", to the effect that "any adequate theory of meaning must enable us to see how the meanings of complex terms may be determined, and thereby explained, by the meanings of their parts" (1999: 33). I agree with Horwich that, in a good sense, this isn't much of a constraint at all: given specifications of what "Socrates", "wise" and "is" mean, it is "simple" to derive a specification of what "Socrates is wise" means, *whatever* it is we take ourselves to be doing in making those specifications. As Horwich puts it, "the compositionality constraint leaves entirely open the metaphysical character of meaning properties" (1999: 35) – leaves open, for example, whether these are properties of, or grounded in, the psychology of speakers, regularities of use, social norms or whatever.

My present point, however, is less to concur in the weakness of the compositionality constraint than to urge that fixation on compositionality is a diversion from the more central business of understanding meaning – of, in effect, addressing its "metaphysical character". One wonders, indeed, if the concern of those with this fixation is with meaning at all, as distinct from the meanings of some rather tricky parts of speech, like adverbial qualifiers, whose precise contributions to the meanings of the sentences in which they occur is deemed problematic. My further point is that this fixation and diversion would have been less likely had attention been paid to domains of non-linguistic meaning where compositionality is either rare or entirely absent – to, for example, the meaning of actions. The significance of my signing some document is not a function of the significance of the various "sub-actions" this involves, like unscrewing my pen.

There is something further that an emphasis on compositionality betrays, something indicated in my opening paragraph when I referred to the *theoretical* projects that characterize so many English-language writings on meaning. I want now to explain that reference and, at the same time, explain the sense in which my ambition in this book is *more* modest than that proclaimed in those writings.

"Theory of Meaning"

My modesty consists in the fact that I am not concerned to devise or defend a Theory of Meaning. The capital letters here indicate that the expression is to be understood in a rather particular way, albeit the one in which it is indeed understood by many contemporary students of meaning. While there are many Theories of Meaning on offer, there is a considerable consensus on the general character and objectives of such a Theory.

To begin with, the task of a Theory is not – or not primarily – to elucidate our pre-theoretical notion of meaning. Rather, "meaning" is itself to be understood as a Theoretical term, one whose sense is not independent of, or prior to, a Theory of Meaning. This is sometimes put by saying that meaning should be thought of as what a Theory of Meaning is a Theory of (McDowell 1976: 42). This remark is intended in the same spirit that "Intelligence is what IQ tests test" is intended by people who want to set aside questions about the bearing of IQ tests on our everyday notion of intelligence. Or the point gets put as an insistence that "meaning" is to be regarded as an *explanatory* term, stipulated or invoked in a Theory that aims to explain certain phenomena. We read, for example, that an "adequate" Theory must "accommodate the explanatory relationship between meaning and use" and so "account for" our use of words through treating meanings as "a species of entity" (Horwich 1999: 6, 46).

Secondly, a Theory of Meaning is an empirical one in that its adequacy is to be measured by its capacity to explain or predict empirical facts. At a minimum, it is typically held, "a [T]heory of [M]eaning for a natural language must at least give the meanings of each of its sentences" (Evans and McDowell 1976: vii–viii): must enable one, that is, to derive for each sentence of the language in question a true statement of the sort "'Schnee ist weiss' means that snow is white", where the language in question is German and the Theoretician's language (the "meta-language") is English. Agreement on this aim spawns a further one. Since a natural language is at least relatively "systematic" and "compositional", a Theory of

Meaning for it will itself have the form of a "deductively connected system" (Dummett 1976: 70) – of, say, axioms and rules that generate statements of what each sentence in the language means. So it will be very much a Theory in the sense of "theory" familiar in the theoretical sciences. It is common, finally, for the devisers of Theories of Meaning to agree upon explanatory aims more ambitious than that, simply, of enabling true statements of sentences' meanings. Michael Dummett, for example, following Davidson, uses "a [T]heory of [M]eaning" as a name for "a theoretical representation of the mastery of an entire language" (1976: 69–70). Others speak of a Theory of Meaning as one central component in a larger Theory whose task is to render people's linguistic behaviour maximally intelligible. The Theory will, for example, exhibit why we should indeed expect a speaker with certain beliefs and desires to have asserted or assented to such-and-such a sentence under such-and-such circumstances.

Although, as indicated, this book modestly prescinds from devising or defending a Theory of Meaning in the sense just sketched, this is not because I bluntly reject such an enterprise (though see Chapter 3). Philosophers, I suppose, are at liberty, moreover, to commandeer the phrase for their preferred purposes and, like it or not, the phrase "theory of meaning" is now heard, in many circles, with a capital "T" and "M". But it is worth emphasizing both the gap that separates modern Theories of Meaning from what used to be understood by "theories of meaning" and the oddness one might expect innocent readers to experience when they discover what the capitalized expression refers to. These innocents must find it odd, for example, to hear a Theory of Meaning being equated with a Theory of "entire language" mastery. Odd, too, to hear that the task of a Theory of Meaning is to determine, for each sentence of a language, what its meaning is. That is like hearing that the task of a theory of moral value is to state, for each action performed in a given society, what its moral value is. Indeed, they must find it odd to hear that a Theory of Meaning is not of linguistic meaning generally, but always of meaning-in-L – of, that is, meaning in German or whatever natural language the Theorist has in his sights. Oddest of all, surely, is the seeming lack of concern, by Theorists, for elucidating our ordinary, non-theoretical notion(s) of meaning – the very notion(s) that the innocent might expect to have illuminated in a book bearing a title *Theory of*

Meaning. That expectation can only be disappointed at the news that meaning is (simply) what the Theory devised in the book is a Theory of. (Compare the disappointment of someone who, hoping that IQ tests will tell him something about intelligence, is told that intelligence is whatever IQ tests test.)

Not so long ago, books with a title like *Theory of Meaning* (e.g. Lehrer and Lehrer 1970) would have focused on competing attempts to "define 'meaning'" or to "analyse the concept of meaning". A theory of meaning would have consisted in precisely such an attempt – in, for example, analysing meaning in terms of "ideas" associated with words or of the intentions with which people utter words. Something of the gap between theory and Theory is nicely illustrated by the way in which the so-called "use theory" of meaning has become the "use Theory". Some contemporary Theorists, as we saw, treat meanings as theoretical postulates to *explain* our use of words. Typically, they give an approving nod in Ludwig Wittgenstein's direction. But they shouldn't. It was not at all Wittgenstein's point, in his remarks on meaning and use, to *explain* use by meaning. He speaks, rather, of the meaning of a word – "for a *large* class of cases", at least – as *being* its use in the language (1969: §43). Far from meaning figuring in a Theoretical explanation of use, the concept of meaning is elucidated in terms of use. "Grammar" – to which remarks on meaning belong – "only describes and in no way explains the use of signs" (1969: §496). Wittgenstein would surely have regarded Theories of Meaning, including "use" Theories, as symptomatic of philosophy's unfortunate urge to model itself on explanatory, scientific enquiry.

So do I, in my modesty, simply ignore Theories of Meaning, and consider only theories of meaning? No, not quite. John McDowell, having told us that meaning is what a Theory of Meaning is a Theory of, nevertheless adds that the Theorist will not be "uncritically employing the notion of meaning" (1976: 42). More generally, many Theorists hold that their Theories are informed by, and may in turn serve to regiment or reconstruct, pre-theoretical (or, at any rate, pre-Theoretical) notions of meaning, even when that is not the main business. Consider, for example, Donald Davidson's conception of a Theory of Meaning as a Theory of Truth, whose aim is at least to derive, for each assertive sentence of the language examined, a correct statement of its truth conditions.

Such a Theory plainly reflects and regiments the thought – familiar from Gottlob Frege (1966) and Wittgenstein's *Tractatus* (1988) – that the idea of meaning is intimately related to that of truth, that to know what a sentence means is, perhaps, to know what makes it true. For another example, the ambition of a Theory of Meaning to pair each sentence with a set of "possible worlds" reflects the thought that a sentence's meaning must be some abstract object, like a "proposition". While, then, I shall not be concerned with Theories of Meaning *per se*, I shall, in Chapter 3 especially, consider some of the characterizations of meaning that, so to speak, lurk behind or alongside some such Theories.

Nor, finally, are my concerns limited to theories of linguistic meaning thought of as elucidations of the concept of meaning. This is partly, of course, because my concerns are not limited to linguistic meaning, but also because not everything I discuss happily falls under a label like "elucidation of a concept". This will become clearer, I hope, if I provide something of a preview of what I shall be discussing.

"Accounts of meaning"

The conclusions of the previous sections might be summarized, in a sloganizing way, by saying that this book is concerned to offer, not a Theory of (linguistic) Meaning, but an account of meaning in general. "Account of meaning" is a conveniently bland label. What should it cover? That is not an easy question to answer. Meaning is one of our "big" notions – big in scope, big in the roles it plays in human thought and conduct, and big with the issues it spawns. The difficulty of "containing" the notion in any relatively cohesive account is, no doubt, one of the attractions of Theory of Meaning. In a bullet-point age that demands transparency of "aims and objectives" and the setting of "achievable targets", the "research project" of devising a systematic procedure for deriving statements of the meaning of each sentence in a language has its appeal.

It would, as just suggested, be too narrow to equate an account of meaning with the elucidation or analysis of the concept of meaning. There are plenty of matters an account should address that do not comfortably fit that description. Someone interested in substantial questions about the meaning of life is not interested – not solely, at least – in analysing the expression "meaning of life" (nor, one might add, in elucidating the meaning of the word "life"). Again, the relevance or otherwise of an artist's intended meaning to the interpretation of his work is not a matter to be settled solely by analysis of "meaning" and "interpretation".

The character of an account of meaning is better indicated by the title of a once famous, now neglected, book of the 1920s, Ogden and Richards's *The Meaning of Meaning* (1923). Here "meaning" should be heard generously: to ask about the meaning of meaning is to ask various questions, corresponding to the various dimensions of that whose meaning is sought. To begin with, it is to ask about the meaning(s) of the word "meaning" and its cognate terms ("mean", "meaningful" etc.). It was this that largely occupied Ogden and Richards, who came up with something like 16 main senses. That later writers came up with much longer and much shorter lists indicates an obvious problem: cataloguing the meanings of "meaning" presupposes an account of just what one is trying to give an account of. One wants to ask, for example, on what grounds it is decided that "emotive" meaning and "cognitive" meaning are meanings in different senses of "meaning". So as to avoid begging questions, it is better to think of enquiry into the meaning(s) of "meaning" as something like a "perspicuous overview" of that term's behaviour. Such an overview would attend to the different linguistic contexts in which it or related terms occur ("I mean to . . .", "By the word '. . .' he means —", "This sentence means that . . .", "That event means —", and so on). But it will also attend to the connections between these uses, without having pre-empted the issue of whether, in these different contexts, "mean" has different meanings or reflects irreducibly different "types" of meaning ("speaker's meaning", "sentence meaning", "natural meaning" etc.). A perspicuous overview would, moreover, attend to the many *domains* in which talk of meaning figures. An account of the meaning(s) of "meaning" would record that it is not only words, sentences and utterances in the linguistic domain that may be described as meaningful, but items in such various domains as those of art, ceremonial, social action and bodily gesture. Again, there should have been no pre-emption of whether, as applied to these various domains, talk of meaningfulness itself bears different meanings. It is into the meaning of "meaning", so construed, that I enquire in Chapter 2.

As anticipated, however, an account of meaning – an enquiry into the meaning of meaning – cannot be confined to an overview of the behaviour of the word "meaning". One reason, to which I return in Chapter 2, is that the enquiry can hardly be one, simply, into a particular word of the English language (and its cognates). An account of meaning knows no national boundaries, yet the English word behaves idiosyncratically: in no other language I know of is there a term that behaves in quite that way. The more important reason is that just as "What is the meaning of love?" may, in virtue of perfectly familiar uses of "meaning", be asking something different from "What is the meaning of the word 'love'?", so it is when "love" is replaced by the term "meaning" itself. The analogy with this other "big" notion, love, is worth pursuing.

"What is the meaning of love?" may be asking about – well, let's call it the *import* of love. What, the question may be, does it show about human beings that they – and only they – can fall in love? What, perhaps, does love intimate? That there is a "spiritual" dimension to human nature, or what? Analogous questions may be asked about the significance of meaning. What does it show about our being-in-the-world that, as Maurice Merleau-Ponty (1962: xix) put it, we are such inveterate "traffickers in meaning", creatures who are "condemned to meaning"? What, if anything, is intimated by our recognition of meanings in the natural world – something "spiritual" behind the order of things, perhaps?

Rather differently, to ask about the meaning of love may be to ask about its meaning *qua* purpose or function. Is love, as such unromantics as Schopenhauer and neo-Darwinians think, just evolution's device for getting us to procreate? Or, as Diotima in the *Symposium* more delicately held, is it there in order to lead us on to appreciation of "higher" things – Beauty and the Good? Again, there are analogous questions to ask about meaning. Is meaning something that "evolved" out of more "primitive" phenomena in response to the communicative needs of sophisticated creatures like us? Or maybe the "functional" questions are about, not love and meaning *per se*, but our explicit and self-conscious deployment of those notions. Why do we not only fall in love, but find it important to speak the language of love? Why are we not simply traffickers in meaning, but creatures who doggedly deploy the notion of meaning when attempting to understand one another and our world?

Finally, to ask about the meaning of love may be to ask, so to speak, about its *status*, to want to know how love may be *placed* in relation to other, somehow connected things so as, it is hoped, to illuminate its nature. Some years ago, there was a vogue for "Love means . . ." posters that people stuck on their bedroom walls, with lines on them like "Love means never having to say you're sorry". Such lines did not "define" the word "love"; rather, they served to locate love, perceptively or otherwise, in relation to such phenomena as jealousy, commitment and regret. Enquiry into the meaning of meaning may, analogously, be seeking illumination via location of status. Such familiar claims as "Meaning is picturing", "Meanings are norms or rules", and "Meaning is use" might be compared to the "Love means . . ." lines on the poster. They locate meaning by, in those three cases, respectively placing it in or close to the orbits of depiction, the law and technology. Just as people can disagree about what should replace the dots in "Love means . . ." (Proust held that love means always being consumed by jealousy), so philosophers may disagree about the light cast by locating meaning in ways like those mentioned.

So an account of meaning, besides providing a perspicuous overview of the behaviour and scope of "meaning" and its cognates, should address the questions about the import, function and status of meaning that I have subsumed under the heading of an enquiry into the meaning of meaning. Does that exhaust the task of an account of meaning? No – consider again the analogy with the notion of love. Someone might, to his own satisfaction at least, have accounted for the import and so on of love, only to find that his account spawns further, characteristically philosophical questions – epistemological, metaphysical, evaluative or whatever. It might, for example, get him worrying about how, if ever, people *know* they are in love, or even about whether, *really*, there is such a thing. Maybe "love" is a sentimental and misleading term for something more basic (in more senses than one) – "sexual chemistry", say. Or it might get him wondering if love is, after all, a good thing: isn't there something to be said for an ascetic life immune to the temptations and turbulence of love? A fuller account of love, then, would not only address the questions of the meaning of love, but address as well the issues or problems that answers to those questions generate.

The same can be said about an account of meaning. Almost any account of the meaning of meaning – of its import, function and status – will spawn "issues". How, if such-and-such a view of meaning is right, do we ever know what words or actions mean? Do we speakers and agents really have the control over the significance of our words and deeds that we imagine? *Really*, *deep down*, is there meaning at all? May it not be a misleading "folk" term for something more basic, like the causal conditions governing the production of certain noises and movements? When we talk about things as meaningful, is this from a merely "subjective" perspective that we should transcend if we want to describe things as they are "in themselves"? Is meaning something that we – especially, perhaps, the artists among us – should strive for, or should we let our poems (as Archibald MacLeish urged) and indeed our lives "just be", rather than mean? So a fuller account of meaning would address such generated issues, not just the questions about the meaning of meaning, answers to which give rise to such issues.

There is no obvious limit to the range of issues that might be spawned, which means that there is no such thing as a complete account of meaning. The most one can do is consider the issues that philosophers have actually found it important to raise, and then exercise one's judgement in deciding which to tackle. (The questions chronicled in the previous paragraph *have*, of course, been raised, by philosophers as various as Saul Kripke, Jacques Derrida, W. V. Quine and Martin Heidegger.) The judgement I exercise in this book may or may not correspond to the reader's own. He or she may judge that this or that issue which I discuss under the heading of "meaning and the arts", say, or "meaning and society" is not the most pressing. But I would hope they agree that the issues on which I focus neither are, nor have struck a wide philosophical constituency as, uninteresting ones.

One implication, incidentally, of there being no obvious limit to the range of issues spawned by enquiry into the meaning of meaning is that it is senseless to speak of *the* problem of meaning. Yet there is a disarming tendency these days to do just that. In particular, one hears that *the* task of a philosophy of meaning is to explain the "amazing", "remarkable", "puzzling" and "mysterious" fact that anything can be meaningful at all (Lycan 2000: 3). One knows, of course, where such talk comes from – from the direction of a scientism or naturalism, touched on earlier, for which the intelligibility of anything not transparently describable and explicable in natural scientific terms is in question. The idea that something so utterly familiar to us as meaningfulness should be "amazing" and peculiarly "mysterious" sounds quaint to me. Indeed, one might think, with Edmund Husserl (e.g. 1970), that a problem almost the reverse of what is alleged to be *the* problem of meaning is the greater one. This is the matter of explaining how, from our familiar descriptions of a meaning-laden "life-world", we ascend – or descend – to relatively "objective" descriptions of a world from which the meaningful has been expelled. If we are inveterate "traffickers in meaning", how do we get out of the traffic? Of course, given that we do aspire to naturalistic descriptions, with some success perhaps, problems about the relationship between the vocabulary of meaning and the vocabulary of science indeed arise, notably in the social sciences (see Chapter 5). But these are just some among the many, highly varied problems spawned by accounts of the meaning of meaning. For some philosophers, they are central; for others, not. Horses for courses, to repeat the old adage.

2 The reach of meaning

The title of this chapter is a pun. In its first section, I want to convey the reach of meaning in the sense of its scope or extent, to draw attention to the many contexts and ways in which, and the many types of item of which, meaning is predicated. There is, however, another, albeit obsolete, sense in which to have the reach of something is to comprehend or get the measure of it. A later section of the chapter, accordingly, attempts a preliminary and general understanding of the phenomenon whose immense scope will already have been indicated. We want, as it were, to get something of very great reach within our reach.

Frames, focuses and fields

One task for an enquiry into the meaning of meaning, we saw in Chapter 1, is to gain a perspicuous overview of the behaviour of "meaning" and cognate and related terms. Here I shall attempt something less ambitious, for even to illustrate, let alone taxonomize, the many ways in which those terms behave would be a long and gruelling job. That writers have turned up 16 or more alleged meanings of "meaning" – and then only in the domain of linguistic meaning – is some indication of the size of that job. (In what follows, I should stress, I do not assume that the distinctions I draw are best described as ones between different senses of "meaning".) My concern is more with the appropriate response to the reach of meaning than to draw a comprehensive map of it.

A good way of getting a feel for the scope of our talk of meaning is to recognize that it varies along three dimensions – those of *frame*, *focus* and *field*, as I shall label them. By "our talk of meaning", I have something fairly precise in mind: sentences which state or indicate what some item, in my broad sense, means – sentences, that is, of the very general form ". . . means —". Such "meaning-indicator" sentences, as I'll call them, can vary according to their more precise grammatical forms (their "frames"), the sorts of indication they provide (their "focuses") and the types of item whose meaning they indicate (their "fields").

Let me begin with frames, confining myself for the time being to the domain of linguistic meaning. Sentences of the form ". . . means —" vary, to begin with, according to the kind of grammatical subject they have. Sentences, individual words, speakers, the linguistic acts performed by speakers can all be said to mean, as can many other items. Hence, what precedes "means" in a meaning-indicator statement may be the name of a sentence, of a word, of a person, and so on. For example, in the statement "John's telling me to shut up meant that —", the grammatical subject refers to a linguistic act performed by John. The frames of meaning-indicators vary, then, according to the type of grammatical subject they contain. "S means —", where "S" is any name of a sentence, is one frame; "A means —", where "A" is any name of a speaker, is another.

But the frames of meaning-indicator statements vary, too, according to what follows "means". This may be a that-clause (". . . means that snow is white"), the name of a sentence (". . . means [the same as] 'Snow is white'"), the name of a concept (". . . means DOG"), the name of a word (". . . means [the same as] 'dog'"), an infinitive (". . . means to warn you off"), the name of a thing (". . . means Paris, France, not Paris, Texas"), and much else. So frames vary according to what, in old-fashioned grammars, are called their grammatical objects. ". . . means that p", where "p" is replaced by a sentence, is one frame; ". . . means to V", where "V" is replaced by a verb, is another.

This is indeed "old-fashioned" grammatical analysis, though the sort you still usually find in dictionaries. It may well be that, at another level of analysis – that of "deep" grammar or logical form – there is not one verb which occurs in both ". . . means that —" and ". . . means to —": rather, we should treat "mean that" and "mean to" as whole expressions that cannot be broken up into "mean" plus "that" or "to". But old-fashionedness doesn't matter in the present context, where the aim is simply to chronicle the variety of word patterns into which the word "mean" may slot.

So frames vary according to their permissible grammatical subjects or objects, or – of course – both. For example, each of the following three meaning-indicators differs from the other two in both respects:

"'Schnee ist weiss' means that snow is white",
"By saying 'Schnee ist weiss', Kurt means (the same as) 'Snow is white'"

and

"'Paris', in this book, means Paris, France"

So much, for the time being, for frames. I now turn to focuses. Consider the following example of a frame:

"When he said 'It's past midnight', John meant that —"

Here are just some of the possible meaning-indicators that share this frame:

"When etc., John meant that it was after 12pm"
"When etc., John meant that it was time to go home"
"When etc., John meant that he was bored stiff"
"When etc., John meant that the new millennium had begun"
"When etc., John meant that the die is cast, that there is no turning back the clock"

These are not simply different indicators of what John meant, for they also reflect very different angles of interest in, different focuses on, his words: their literal content, their pragmatic purpose, their expressive significance, their "deeper" import, their metaphorical thrust, or whatever. Notice that the indicators need not compete. Indeed, they may all be true: John *did* state that it was after 12pm, *was* urging people to go home and expressing his boredom with the party and he was *also* conveying that it was a momentous time – the beginning of a new millennium and the occasion to make a new beginning in life.

Or consider, as another example, the frame:

"By saying 'The food is delicious', Karen meant to —"

Inter alia, she may have meant to inform her friends how good the food was, pay a compliment to the chef, encourage him to cook the same again, express her gastronomic pleasure, mock the chef (Karen is an ironist), or say "The food is delicate" (English is not Karen's first language). Karen may have meant to do any one of these things, and perhaps several of them at once, but again the focuses on what she meant, manifested by these indicators, are very different. One indicator focuses on the content of her words, another on the kind of speech act she was performing, another on some further purpose she had and so on.

Focus is not a notion that lends itself to precise definition and nor, for the time being at least, am I concerned with the taxonomy of focuses. It's enough, for the present, to register the fact that, when indicating what words or utterances or speakers mean, we do so with many distinct interests and concerns in mind. Our focus on one occasion or in one context may be quite different on or in another.

Let me end with the last of the three Fs – fields of meaning. The term "fields" is designed to register the variety in the kinds of item that may be said to mean. Which items are allocated to which fields, and how narrow or wide these fields are, depends on our classificatory interests. One might, for example, count all sentences as constituting a field of their own; or one might treat sentences, words and other linguistic expressions as constituting some larger field. A wider field still is obtained by adding in what Roland Barthes (1968: 11) calls those "larger fragments of discourse" that, in his view, semantics, but not semiology, tends to ignore – para-graphs, stories, newspaper articles and so on. One could proceed, if so wished, to the mega-field of linguistic meaning, encompassing bits of language (of whatever size), linguistic acts, speakers of language – anything, in effect, that may be said to mean through either being or using a linguistic item.

As emphasized in Chapter 1, the mega-field of linguistic mean-ing, however vast, could not be the only field of meaning. The reach of meaning extends well beyond language, even in a relaxed sense of "language" that includes, say, Morse code and dance notation. Non-linguistic signs and gestures can, as much as words or sentences, mean that —, mean (the same as) another and mean some object. Agents of non-linguistic acts can, as much as speakers, mean to — and mean that — by their acts. ("When the kids jump into my arms", remarked a survivor of 11 September, "it has a whole different meaning.") Silent and unscripted ceremonies, rituals and family Christmas traditions lend themselves to talk of meaning – to meaning-indication – no less than speeches and newspaper cuttings. Non-verbal artworks and other cultural products attract the vocabulary of meaning as naturally as their linguistic cousins. One may, remarks Wittgenstein (1969: §533), be brought to "comprehend" a musical theme – to have its "meaning . . . explained". Meanings, we are reminded in a book called *The Meaning of Gardens*, "saturate" and "reside in" gardens (Francis & Hester 1990: 8, 46).

In that same book, we also encounter many different styles of meaning-indication – ranging from remarks on the mythological and religious meanings of gardens in a bygone age to ones on the garden as a "representation" of what is at once constant and ever-changing in nature. Such remarks illustrate the fact that meaning-indicators of non-linguistic items may, like those of a speaker's words, vary in focus. A section of a piece of music may express a mood, contribute in a significant way to the structure of the whole piece, intimate something to the audience, refer to another piece of music, and so on. Each of these indications of the meaning of the section of music reflects a distinct focus upon it. Non-linguistic items of meaning also, and obviously, share with linguistic ones that their division into fields is an elastic matter and a function of our classificatory interests. For certain purposes, for example, one may treat the categories that semiologists enjoy devising – signals, indexes, icons, symbols and the like – as constituting distinct fields; or one might, towards the other extreme, lump them all together into a field of non-linguistic "signifiers". Again, for certain purposes, it may be useful to construct fields that contain both linguistic and non-linguistic items. Verbal utterances and gestures, after all, share features that, from certain perspectives, relevantly distinguish them from, say, paintings or ceremonies.

Bland and elastic as talk of fields of meaning is, it is potentially misleading – and in a way that may blind one to the true reach of meaning. Such talk may encourage the thought that only certain items (words, pictures, ceremonies etc.) – ones made for the part, as it were, and nicely allocatable to this or that field – belong within the reach of meaning. But this would be a mistake: *anything at all* may, in an appropriate context, be spoken of as having meaning or significance – from the cup in front of me to the cat sitting beside me, from the clouds I see through the window to the window I see them through. Just as a terrain may contain, but extend beyond, the fields that have been cultivated upon it, so the terrain of meaning extends beyond the fields of made-to-measure items recently illustrated. Is there a name for that terrain? We might call it "the world" in the sense made familiar by phenomenologists, such as Heidegger and Merleau-Ponty – the "human world" or "life-world", the world of things and events as, so to speak, taken up into and related to our lives. One of Merleau-Ponty's expressions for that world is, interestingly, "the cradle of meanings" (1962: 430).

This point about the universality of meaning or significance, which plays an important role in this book, will be elaborated in due course. For the moment, I confine myself to briefly indicating what I do, and do not, have in mind by it. But first, a methodological point. In Chapter 1, I remarked that a philosophical enquiry into meaning cannot consist, simply, in an enquiry into the word "meaning" – not least because that English word has no exact correspondence to any word in any other language with which I am familiar. Germans, for example, employ several words, not always interchangeably – including *Sinn* and *Bedeutung* – where we, more parsimoniously, make do with "meaning". More relevantly, "meaning" and "significance" are not colloquially interchangeable, in all contexts, in English; whereas, in French and Spanish, for example, the word most commonly translated as "meaning" is also their word for "significance" or a close cognate. The relevance of this point is as follows: colloquially, it is more common, in English, to speak of the significance of artefacts, natural objects and so on than of their meaning. Across the Channel, no such difference obtains. Since it is a contingent quirk that "meaning" is used more restrictively than its nearest equivalents in French and Spanish, it is one that for the most part, at least, we should ignore. In other words, to gauge the reach of meaning, we should attend to the use of the English word "significance" and its cognates as well as to that of "meaning"; otherwise, our enquiry into meaning-cum-significance may be arbitrarily stunted. (Could the tendency of English-language semanticists immediately to think of meaning in connection, primarily, with language, while French semiologists think of meaning-cum-significance in connection with much wider phenomena, be a reflection of this quirk?)

Here are two things I do *not* have in mind when saying that anything in the world may mean. First, the point is not the barely contestable one that anything may have meaning conferred upon it – as when the retired general, reliving one of his battles, makes the salt-cellar stand for an enemy regiment, the spoon represent GHQ and so on; or as when an avant-garde artist exhibits a lump of Blu-Tack or elephant dung and predictably prompts the art world to ponder its meaning. What happens, in such cases, is, in effect, the transformation of an *objet trouvé* into an item belonging to some familiar field of meaning – that of symbols, artworks or whatever. Secondly, the point is not, at the other extreme, the plainly contestable one – despite its popularity in medieval and Renaissance times – that the world is "the Book of God", a vast repository of "signs" replete with "messages" for those with the hermetic powers to discern them. Modern scientists and philosophers who think it a great advance that the natural world has become "disenchanted" – that objects and events are no longer "explained" in terms of the messages they send – may be right. But it is quite illegitimate for them to draw the conclusion that talk of the meaning and significance of "mere" things is therefore generally to be excluded.

Certainly it is nothing "occult" or "enchanted" that I intend in speaking of the terrain or "cradle" of meaning. I have in mind such simple and familiar contexts, in which talk of meaning is perfectly natural, as the following. An archaeologist, on digging up a lump of clay, asks, "Does this have any significance?" – to which his colleague may reply, "Yes, it's a cup", or "No, it's just a bit of soil". A traveller asks his companion, "Do those clouds over the mountain mean anything?" – to which the reply may be "Yes, they do: there's going to be a real storm", or "No, they're always there at this time of year". I postpone until later consideration of what is involved when, in the affirmative answers, meaning or significance is attributed to these "mere" things – the cup, the clouds or whatever. But it is not hard to see, in the broadest terms, what is involved: an indication, however implicit, of how these "mere" things are taken up into a world of human concerns and practices.

Taxonomy and regimentation

What should be the response of the philosophical enquirer to the reach of meaning – to the variety of frames, focuses and fields just rehearsed? One response, already met with in Chapter 1, is that of marked indifference. This is the response of the Theorist of Meaning, for whose purposes "meaning" gets its sole relevant sense through its role in a Theory devised for some explanatory end, such as accounting for "mastery of an entire language". While the decision to commandeer the particular word "meaning" may have been suggested by some familiar use it has, its employment by the Theorist, once commandeered, is no longer answerable to everyday, pre-Theoretical understanding. References to expressive or emotive meaning, for example, should no more constrain the Theory than references to military or argumentative force should constrain the physicist's Theory of Force.

At the other extreme is the response of the pure taxonomist. What the reach of meaning calls for is a full, careful and elegant classification that does justice to the variety in our talk of meaning along the axes of the three Fs. Many authors have busied themselves with such taxonomizing. Corresponding to the different meaning-indicator frames I catalogued, there have been set up such categories as "sentence meaning", "speaker's meaning", "utterance meaning" and "dictionary meaning". Corresponding to the various focuses of meaning I illustrated, such categories as "literal meaning", "cognitive meaning", "emotive meaning", "performative meaning" and "figurative meaning" have been devised. And parallel to some of the fields of meaning I distinguished, taxonomists have spoken of "linguistic meaning", "pictorial meaning", "natural meaning", "non-natural meaning", "iconic meaning" and so on. The dedicated taxonomist will, of course, do more than simply draw up a long list. Like his opposite number in botany, he will want to order the items, to avoid cross-categorization and to erect something like a structure of genera, species and sub-species.

Another common response to the reach of meaning lies somewhere between those of the Theorist and the mere taxonomist. *Regimenters*, as we may call them, want to pay more respect to our everyday talk of meaning than does the Theorist. They view their job as being to "capture" and explicitly articulate pre-theoretical conceptions of meaning and, regimented as their account of meaning is, it must be sensitive to these conceptions. But "capturing", they will add, goes beyond pure taxonomy, for the latter fails to provide a general understanding of what it is that is being taxonomized and categorized. Exposure of the meaning(s) of meaning requires, to recall the terms used in Chapter 1, more than a "perspicuous overview"; it must also address questions about the import, role and status of meaning.

Regimentation, typically, goes in three stages. First, the regimenter – often in Draconian style – excludes from his purview various frames, focuses and fields. Without such exclusions, he is confident, there is no prospect for anything like a general account of meaning, for some uses and applications of "meaning" are just too idiosyncratic and special. These are the ones, conveniently, which he thinks are anyway unproblematic: ones where talk of meaning is anyway and easily paraphrasable in other terms. "Those clouds mean rain" and "His words meant that he was bored", for example, may be excluded, since these can be paraphrased in ways that show how accidental and inessential the occurrence of "mean" in these sentences is. They may be paraphrased, roughly, as "Those clouds are nearly always followed by rain" and "His words were a symptom of boredom". Secondly, having reduced the reach of meaning, the regimenter identifies among the remaining, bona fide meaning-indicators one or a few that, in his judgement, have priority. *These*, he holds, are the paradigmatic statements of meaning on which to concentrate. Finally, the regimenter proceeds to explain the "secondary", non-paradigmatic notions of meaning in terms of the "primary", prioritized one(s).

Here is one well-known exercise in regimentation. First, exclude cases of so-called "natural meaning" ("Those clouds mean rain" and so on). Secondly, prioritize frames of the form "By doing/saying X, A means that —", and elucidate what such meaning-indicators assert (e.g. that, by doing or saying X, A intends his audience to believe that —). Finally, show how further, "secondary" talk about meaning derives from this paradigmatic kind (e.g. show that the meanings of sentences or conventional gestures can be understood in terms of what people standardly mean/intend by producing them). This is a crude summary of H. P. Grice's (1989: Ch. 14) approach to meaning – of what is called, in a phrase that indicates its regimental character, "the Gricean programme" (to which I return in Chapter 3).

Regimentation is less cavalier than the Theorist's indifference and more interesting than mere taxonomy. But doubts can arise about each stage in the regimental procedure. Some, perhaps all, of the exclusions made may be too hasty. Maybe "mean" in "Those clouds mean rain" is not occurring "accidentally" and in a way that invites paraphrase into a quite different idiom. Moreover, both exclusion and prioritizing may reflect theoretical predilections and ambitions that enquiry into the meaning of meaning – and not into something else – is better off without. Jerry Fodor (2001: 7), for example, may be right to insist that – when dealing with both language and thought – "questions of content need to be distinguished from questions of use". But that hardly warrants his verdict of "a perfectly awful idea" on Wittgenstein's (alleged) "conflation" of "the meaning of an expression with what it can do, or be used to do". The verdict betrays a pre-emptive exclusion of the relevance to an account of meaning of such familiar meaning-indicators as

"'The food is delicious' means that one greatly enjoyed the food"

and

"On that night, 'It's past midnight' meant something momentous – the dawn of a new age"

Fodor or whoever is perfectly entitled, for his purposes, to focus on "content" – the sort of thing, presumably, indicated by "'It's past midnight' means that it is past midnight" – rather than "use". He is not entitled, however, to register that predilection by condemning, as "perfectly awful", attention to meaning-indicators that focus on use.

Or consider the now pervasive prioritizing of sentence-meaning over word-meaning, of frames in which what precedes "means" is the name of a sentence, not an individual word. While there may be some truth, on some interpretation of it, in the elastic Fregean maxim that words only have meaning in the context of sentences, it is clear that what inspires this prioritizing is the fixation on "compositionality" discussed in Chapter 1. (On this maxim and fixation, see Baker and Hacker 1980: Ch. 8.) If the "real" job of a Theory of Meaning is to specify sentence-meanings in a way that displays their compositional character, references to word-meanings, if made at all, will only be of interest because of the contribution made to realizing that ambition. But why think that this is the "real" job, or the only one that matters?

It should be a cause of further concern that different regimenters prioritize such different meaning-indicators. For one author, pride of place belongs to the frame

"S means that p",

where "p" is either the very sentence named by "S" or one translationally equivalent to it. For example,

"'Snow is white' means that snow is white"

or

"'Schnee ist weiss' means that snow is white"

For, so it is argued, it is in the "objective truth conditions" stated in such indicators that we find "the key to meaning" (Davidson 1986a: 307). For another author, since "the key to meaning" – a popular expression – is located in what speakers or agents intend, priority is given to such frames as

"By saying/doing . . ., A means to —"

(Searle 1983: 27). For other authors – structuralists in the tradition of Saussure – priority is given to frames in which a signifier, such as a word, is explicitly related to other signifiers: for example, "W means almost the opposite of W*". For this registers their contention that "the key to meaning" is a system of "differences" among signifiers.

The suspicion will be growing that this variety of prioritizations is due to competing theoretical ambitions – or if not to these, exactly, then to large-scale and competing background conceptions. Here I have in mind, for example, the very different prioritizations that reflect what Charles Taylor has called the "designative" and "expressive" conceptions of meaning (1985: Ch. 10) – according to which meaning is respectively conceived as what meaningful items stand for and as what belongs to activities in so far as they show something about us, the agents.

Finally, with all the proposals with which I am acquainted, there are well-documented difficulties in employing the "key to meaning" which has been designed to fit the prioritized frames, focuses or fields, in order then to gain access to further ones. One thinks, for example, of the problems that "the Gricean programme" encounters in defining the conventional meanings of sentences in terms of speakers' intended meanings, which may be very unconventional. Sometimes, indeed, such difficulties simply lead to a new round of exclusions. How, asks Davidson, for example, can metaphorical meaning be accommodated by an account of meaning in terms of "objective truth conditions"? Answer: it cannot, so there is no such thing as metaphorical meaning (1984: Essay 17). In other words, statements like "By 'It's past midnight', John meant that there is no turning back" are excluded from the field of genuine meaning-indicators. (I discuss this view of metaphorical (non)-meaning in Chapter 6.)

In the following section, I sketch a general account of meaning that does not pre-emptively exclude any of our familiar talk about meaning and does not assume that any particular segment of such talk has priority. The policy of non-exclusion reflects the presumption that it is neither an accident nor the result of illegitimate conceptual conflations that the same word "mean" occurs in the many contexts I have indicated. None of these occurrences can safely, and in advance, be excluded as irrelevant to enquiry into the meaning of meaning. Presumptions of that kind are, to be sure, defeasible. It is often argued, for example, that application of the term "law" both to natural regularities and to institutional or moral norms is rooted in the failure of ancient peoples properly to distinguish between the natural and cultural orders. It is not implausible, certainly, to think that the student of the laws of nature may safely exclude from his remit the laws of Justinian or Manu. But I see no compelling reason to think that the situation is the same with "meaning". (Actually there is a verb "mean", in use in Scotland and related to "moan" and "mourn", with the sense of "complain". An account of meaning may indeed ignore uses of that verb, but it only has to be mentioned for the difference between it and the uses of "mean" which I have been discussing to be apparent.) The policy of not assuming priorities is also defeasible: maybe an account of the meaning of meaning will reveal that, for example, the possibility of some frames, focuses or fields of meaning depends upon that of others. But it would be quite wrong to start with confident, dogmatic assertions to the effect that, for instance, this or that particular style of meaning-indication is the real, essential or key one.

Meaning, explanation and life

"The hermeneutical *Urphänomen*", writes Hans-Georg Gadamer (1977: 11), is that "assertions can only be understood" as "answer[s] to question[s]". This may be exaggerated, but it draws attention to something important – that the primary role of hermeneutical assertions or, in my terminology, meaning-indicators is the practical one of answering questions about how somebody or something (a word, a gesture or whatever) is to be understood. It is here, "in the stream of life", as Wittgenstein puts it (1975: §173) – in the practical business of explanation, of averting misunderstanding – that talk about meaning has its natural home. And it is Wittgenstein who provides the motto for what I want to emphasize over the next few pages: "if you want to understand the use of the word 'meaning', look for what are called 'explanations of meaning'" (1969: §560). Differently expressed: enquiry into the meaning of meaning should attend to what count as explanations of meaning.

"The importance of this truism" – that "meaning is what is given by explanations of meaning" – cannot, remark two sensitive commentators on Wittgenstein, "be overestimated" (Baker and Hacker 1980: 35). The "truism" is important, not least because it reminds us how peculiar it is for philosophers of language to prioritize and obsessively concentrate upon meaning-indicators of kinds that can barely play a role in explaining to anyone what somebody or something may have meant – indicators like "'Snow is white' means that snow is white" and "'Dog' means DOG". This is to concentrate on the vocabulary of meaning when it is "on holiday", not when invoked "in the stream of life". If, in general, we come to understand words by grasping their uses and roles, why should it be different with words like "meaning" and "significance" in particular?

It goes without saying that the relationship between meaning and explanation emphasized by Wittgenstein is not at all the one perceived or, rather, stipulated by some Theorists of Meaning. For them, as we saw in Chapter 1, meanings are theoretical postulates employed to explain our use of words. Wittgenstein's is the entirely different idea that the notion of meaning is to be understood through reflection on what count as explanations of meaning. The explanations he has in mind are not those that Theories furnish, but ones which "serve . . . to remove or avert a misunderstanding" about particular words, gestures or whatever (1969: §87).

Two proposals, then, inform my discussion of the meaning of meaning. First, we should regard meaning-indicators – with their various frames, focuses and fields – as belonging to the general practice of offering explanations of meanings. (Note that even "'Snow is white' means that snow is white" *might* play such a role. It could serve, for example, to correct someone who thinks that "Snow is white" is an idiom, like "The grass is always greener . . .". "No," one explains, "it means just what it appears to mean – that snow is white, *period*.") Secondly, we should understand the meaning of meaning through concentrating on what it is to explain meanings. If this understanding is to be at all general and unified, we must attempt something not explicitly essayed by Wittgenstein himself, even if he offers hints as to how the attempt might proceed. Wittgenstein is seemingly content simply to point to certain activities – ostension, for example, or describing how something is learnt – and to say "*These* are what count as explanations of meaning", without elaborating on what makes them thus count. In the remainder of this chapter, I want to say something of a general kind about explanations of meaning, and hence about the meaning of meaning. (The generality of what I say inevitably makes for a blandness and looseness that, I hope, is removed in subsequent chapters.)

An unadventurous, yet important, start is to remark that, whatever else it is to explain an item's meaning, it is to connect the item to something outside or larger than itself, to locate it in relation to what is – in either of those ways – "beyond" itself. It was, reflects a character in *The God of Small Things*, as she surveys the objects in a room, the "disconnected . . . isolated things that didn't *mean* anything" for her, as though "the intelligence that . . . connects . . . [were] suddenly lost" (Roy 1998: 226). When people ask what an item means, it is a request for such a connection or location to be provided. This relatively banal point is sufficient to distinguish explanation of meaning from at least some other species of explanation. One does not, for example, explain some object's meaning when one explains its behaviour in terms of its physical constitution. (Nor, one might add, does one explain a sentence's meaning by exposing its compositional features – though this may explain how it has the meaning it does.) Still, there are plenty of explanations that connect things to what is "beyond" them that are not explanations of meaning. Examples would include explaining an event in terms of what caused it and explaining the course of a river in topological terms.

Two questions, clearly, must be addressed if explanations of meaning are to be distinguished from these and other forms of explanation. First, to what do explanations of meaning – meaning-indicators – relate items? What, in the case of all such explanations, is the "beyond" – the "permanent subject", to use Wilhelm Dilthey's expression (1979: 220) – to which they connect items? Secondly, what is the character of the relation or connection indicated? How does it differ from other relations to the "beyond", such as causal ones?

In addressing the first question, I take my lead from Dilthey. Meaning, he writes, is a matter of "belonging to a whole". That "whole" is what he calls "Life": hence, something is meaningful "in so far as it . . . signifies . . . something that is part of Life" (1979: 233, 236). Dilthey cites musical meaning both as an analogy for and as an instance of the general phenomenon of meaning. Just as a musical phrase only has meaning through its place in a larger whole, such as a melody, so quite generally something is meaningful only in virtue of its relation to Life as a whole. But this general point applies to the musical phrase itself: proximally, one might say, it has meaning as part of a melody, but ultimately through its place, however modest, in Life. For a melody is not a mere sequence of sounds; it is something people play and listen to, something possible only in relation to a certain cultural practice and sensibility. By "Life", Dilthey does not, of course, intend the sum total of what is living or the biosphere. Life is what he elsewhere, like Wittgenstein after him, calls a *Lebensform* – a "form of life". It is akin to Husserl's "Life-world" and to the "human world" spoken of by Heidegger and other phenomenologists.

For the present, we can leave this notion of Life or a form of life blandly unspecific, and think of it as a set of very general, very basic shared practices that constitute the framework to which, Dilthey and his followers maintain, all assignments of meaning eventually refer. Here, to be a little more specific, are some of the activities that Wittgenstein mentions as parts of a given form of life: giving and obeying orders, reporting and describing, hoping and dreading, telling stories, asking and praying (1969: §23 and p. 174).

To provide explanations of meaning, I suggest, is to respond to actual or potential questions about the relationship of items (utterances, gestures, rituals or whatever) to Life, about their location in the framework that enables the possibility of significance. That relationship or location is what the questioner has yet to grasp. This suggestion invites, however, an obvious objection. "Certainly", the objection goes

> people – especially anthropologists – sometimes explain the meaning or significance of something by explicitly indicating its contribution to or place within some very general cultural practice. But that is the exception, not the rule. Typically, explanation of the meaning of an utterance or a gesture involves nothing so ambitious and "grand" as laying bare aspects of a whole form of life. So it is quite wrong to see any essential connection between explanations of meaning and Life.

Dilthey would agree with the objector – up until the final sentence. In providing "elementary" understanding and explanation, he remarks, "we do not go back to the whole context of Life which forms the permanent subject" of meaning (1979: 220). We do not, because we have no need to. But this is so only because the "elementary" explanation provided typically engages with the questioner's implicit background understanding. For example, it would be sufficient, typically, in order to enlighten someone puzzling over the significance of the movements made by two people spied from a distance, to tell him that they are shaking hands. But this only enlightens him if he knows that shaking hands is a gesture of greeting, farewell or reconciliation – which, in turn, is something he can know only if he understands a form of life in which such activities are intelligible. Or consider, in this context, Wittgenstein's remarks on ostensive definition. Their point is not, as some commentators imagine, to deny that ostension may explain the meaning of a term, but to emphasize how much understanding on the questioner's part is presupposed by the success of an ostensive explanation. Thus, "one has already to know (or be able to do) something in order to be capable of asking a thing's name" (1969: §31). And this is to know a great deal: a whole background against which our various practices of giving names to people, places and so on are set.

Or consider, too, the nested explanations, described by Heidegger, that may be invited by questions about the significance of items of "equipment", such as hammers. The hammer is there in order to drive in nails; this is done in order to fix some planks together; that, in turn, is done in order to support a structure. All of this, moreover, has a "towards-which" in the form of some desired result, like a new building. Heidegger then points out that while citing any particular "in order to" or "towards-which" might serve to answer a query about an item's or activity's significance, this is possible only in virtue of the questioner's understanding of something more "primary": "the 'for-the-sake-of-which'" with which every meaningful item or activity is "involved" (1980: §§15 and 18). This "for-the-sake-of-which" is "the Being of *Dasein*": that is, our sort of being, human being, which, as Heidegger makes clear, is to be understood – at least in its ordinary "everydayness" – in terms of basic, shared purposes and practices, of a whole culture in effect (the sort, for example, that make *building* things an intelligible activity).

These considerations indicate that Life, the "permanent subject" of meaning, is also its "permanent background". That aspects of this background need only rarely to be exposed when explaining meanings should not blind one to the crucial role they play in the success of all such explanations. Indeed, failure to attend to this background – failure to connect meanings to Life – is responsible for the shallowness of some conceptions of meaning. These are shallow in the way that accounts of some art-form, like lithography, or some game, like football, are shallow when they fail to bring out what makes something an art-form or a game. Certainly a description of the lithographical process or of the rules of football may successfully explain to an ignorant enquirer what lithography or football is – but only if the enquirer already understands what artistic practice or game-playing is, an understanding that requires a larger appreciation of the Life-world in which such activities have an intelligible place.

Consider the shallowness, for example, of the following familiar account of so-called "indirect" or "oblique" meaning, such as ironic meaning: the indirect meaning of an utterance is a proposition, different from that standardly meant by the words, that the speaker intended to communicate. Certainly "By saying 'The food is delicious', Karen meant that the food was terrible" may successfully explain to an enquirer what Karen meant – but not if the enquirer is the young child of glumly unironic parents or an intruder from an alien culture where irony is unknown. The child or alien would not be able to see how Karen, unless she'd simply used the wrong word, *could* mean the opposite of what she said. Nor is the practice of irony some hived-off one that could be adequately explained to the uninitiated without invoking the wider cultural practices – including mockery, social inclusion and exclusion, and humour – that the possibility of irony requires. (See Sperber 1975a and Cooper 1986: Ch. 3.) Like any account of any dimension of meaning, the above conception of "indirect" meaning is shallow when it fails to relate meanings to Life.

Appropriateness

Bland as this talk of Life has been, let us proceed on the assumption that all explanations of meaning relate meaningful items, if only implicitly, to that "permanent subject" or background. I now address the second question, concerning the character of this relation. Clearly it needs addressing. Eating and breathing are related to Life, as necessary conditions of it; but this is not to explain the meaning of eating and breathing. The reason, note, is not that eating and breathing are the wrong sort of items to be spoken of as meaningful. In the Indian regiment's officers' mess, we read in *The Glass Palace*, "every mouthful had a meaning – each represented an advance towards the evolution of a new, more complete kind of Indian" (Ghosh 2000: 278–9). One can sensibly speak, too, of the significance of some Yogic respiratory feat. It is not that eating and breathing cannot be meaningful, but that being a necessary causal condition of Life is not the right sort of relation to Life for conferring meaning.

Let me approach the question indirectly by first glancing at another question, over which much ink has been recently spilt: is meaning a *normative* notion? Some claim that it is, including Saul Kripke, who rejects any account of what it is to understand a given term's meaning if it fails to tell me how I *ought* to apply it (1982: 24). For critics of this claim, however, it rests on the mistaken view that, just because a concept has normative implications, it is itself a normative one. (See, e.g., Horwich 1999: Ch. 8.) It may well be, the critic concedes, that, in a genuinely normative sense, one *ought* to apply terms to what, given their meanings, they actually apply to. But that can be explained by invoking a moral or pragmatic principle of truth-seeking or truth-telling: there is no need, in addition, to invest the notion of meaning with normative force.

I don't myself care too much about the resolution of this debate, since I don't much like the terms in which the issue is being posed. The dispute has been posed as one between those for whom "meanings are invoked to explain how it is *correct* or *appropriate* to use words and sentences, how one *ought* to deploy them", and those for whom they are invoked to explain something "sparer", such as regularities in speech behaviour (Brandom 2000: 185). So characterized, the dispute is one between Theorists of Meaning, disagreeing about the explanatory role to be played by meanings within a Theory of Meaning. When posed in those terms, the issue reflects opposing Theoretical predilections or stipulations.

Still, Brandom's reference to *appropriateness* does hint at something important, and I want to harness this notion to my proposal that meaning be understood in terms of explanations of meaning. (Explanations of meaning "in the stream of life", that is, not explanations that "invoke" or postulate meanings to account for something or other.) "Appropriateness", indeed, will be an apposite term for the relationship between meaningful items and

Life to which, I suggested, explanations of meaning always pertain.

Let's take another person – this time, a stranger in our midst – puzzled at the movements made by two people he spies from a distance.

"Does what they are doing mean anything?", he asks.

"Yes," comes the reply, "they're shaking hands".

"And what's the significance of that?", he continues.

"They're making it up after a fight", he is told.

"'Making it up'? In my society only women can do that. What can it mean for two men to 'make it up'? Men always fight it out to the end!"

"Well, you see, in *our* society, men too are encouraged to bury the hatchet, as we say. That means that they pledge, in future, not to . . .".

In this little exchange, each reply explains the meaning of something that the questioner does not grasp. It does so, we can say, by indicating the appropriateness of what is being questioned. Those movements are appropriate for shaking hands; a handshake is, through convention and tradition, an appropriate gesture of reconciliation; that gesture is appropriate in the context of certain purposes and cultural norms, of aspects of a form of life.

I want to say that all explanations of meaning indicate appropriateness. This doesn't mean that the explanations of the handshake should be taken as a model: explanations of meaning are too various for any single case to serve as a model. But they vary according to the different ways in which items can be appropriate and in which appropriateness can be indicated. (Typically, moreover, and for the reason given in the previous section, the explainer does not need – as in the handshake example – explicitly to "go back to the whole context of Life". An enquirer's background understanding generally makes that otiose.) For another example of meaning-explanation, where a different mode of appropriateness is indicated, think of Heidegger's hammers. The reason that citing the "in-order-to" of a hammer – banging in nails – explains the significance of hammers is that it indicates the appropriate employment of this tool. After all, someone who employs it thus has himself "appropriated this equipment" in a "suitable" manner (1980: 69). One is brought to understand the significance of a tool by being told how it is appropriately, rather than generally, used. (The two need not be the same. In wartime, hammers may be used as makeshift weapons more frequently than as nail-bangers.)

It is not too difficult to see how at least some explanations of linguistic meaning serve to indicate the appropriateness of a linguistic item to what is "beyond" it – ultimately, to Life itself. Elaboration of this is for Chapter 3 where, *inter alia*, I discuss competing views about the appropriateness involved in indications of sentence-meaning. It is more difficult to discern how certain other explanations of meaning invite talk of appropriateness. I have especially in mind so-called "natural" meaning. When someone says "Those clouds mean rain" or "Her long face meant she was depressed", how can he be construed as indicating what is appropriate to what? Isn't he simply remarking on a regularity? Clouds are not appropriate or inappropriate to rain, nor is a long face – unless intentionally drawn to convey one's mood – appropriate or inappropriate to depression. It's simply that there are regular associations here.

However, we should surely pause to consider why, if "Those clouds mean rain" is equivalent to "Clouds of that sort are regularly followed by rain", we don't confine ourselves to saying the latter. Why, that is, do we deploy the idiom of meaning at all? Someone might reply that that idiom is a leftover from the days when people believed that natural phenomena are created by God for a communicative purpose, as so many signs in His "Book". But this speculation is both implausible and unnecessary. Clearly, there are plenty of "merely" natural items that, theology aside, possess significance. A stranger, on seeing children gathering horse-chestnuts, asks, "Do those nuts have some significance for people here?" "Yes," comes the reply, "they're used in a game called conkers. You drill a hole in them, and . . .". So the fact that something is not an artefact – made neither by us nor by God, for some purpose – does not exclude its meaningfulness. Nor would it be relevant to remark, "Ah! So horse-chestnuts are not *intrinsically* meaningful. It's only because they're used for something that they're significant in a way that other nuts aren't." A similar remark could be made about words. (Of course, if one identifies a word, not in phonological or orthographic terms but as a meaningful unit of language, then meaning is built into it, made "intrinsic" to it. But the same can be done by identifying what the children play with, not as horse-chestnuts, but as conkers.)

Horse-chestnuts are significant because they are appropriate for a game: they have, one might say, been appropriated for the purpose of playing that game, been taken up into Life and made "our own". (Recall Heidegger's connection between understanding the significance of hammers and "suitably appropriating" them in using them.) Clouds and (non-deliberate) facial expressions cannot, of course, be appropriated in the same fashion – picked up, manipulated, drilled and so on. But they, too, can be appropriated, taken up into "the stream of life". They can do so by being given a role in our practical activities, as signs or signals. "Do those clouds above the mountain have any significance?" and "Does she always look like that, or does her expression mean something?" are questions at home in contexts where appropriate decisions are to be taken – to keep climbing or to turn back, to ignore or to comfort her. "Yes, they mean an electric storm is on the way" or "Yes, that look means she's deeply depressed": these are meaning-indicators that indicate not the appropriateness of clouds or looks to anything but the appropriateness of our responding in a certain way. That we can treat natural items as signs, thereby appropriating them for our practical purposes, is possible, of course, only because of their regular association with what they signify. But it quite misses the point of, and leaves opaque, the application to natural items of the vocabulary of significance to suppose that "Those clouds mean rain" etc. are simply statements of regularities or causal connections.

The idea of meaning-explanations as indications of appropriateness may, then, be extended to the seemingly recalcitrant field of "merely" natural items. There remain, of course, many kinds of meaningful item, and many frames and focuses of meaning, where elaboration is required in order to see how the idea of appropriateness may illuminate the character of the pertinent meaning-explanations. I try to provide some elaboration in subsequent chapters, but conclude the present one with a brief discussion of its bearing on the questions encountered by an account of meaning that were listed at the end of Chapter 1.

I referred there to the "import", "function" and "status" of meaning as matters that an enquiry into the meaning of meaning should address. My proposals in the present chapter suggest, however, that questions about these matters are not to be answered in quite the style that, I imagine, was originally anticipated. The hope was, I suspect, that the phenomenon of meaning would be assigned some relatively specific import, function and status. But that hope is dashed by reflections on the universal reach of meaning and the variety of its dimensions. Just about anything may, in context, be questioned for its significance, and the diversity of what is indicated by explanations of meaning is apparent from the many frames, focuses and fields of those explanations. This diversity did not entail that "meaning" is ambiguous – Scottish "moaning" and "mourning" aside (see p. 28) – since all meaning-explanations, I urged, serve to indicate the appropriateness of an item to Life. That, if you like, tells us about the status of meaning, but not – as some may have hoped – by locating meaning within some circumscribed orbit like that of "depiction", "law" or "technology", as mooted in Chapter 1. The point is not that one never explains an item by indicating what it represents, a rule that governs its behaviour or a use to which it is put. But these should be seen as different ways, and by no means the only ones, of indicating the appropriateness of an item to Life.

Turning to the question of the function of meaning, that can be summarily answered if construed as one about the function of the concept of meaning, or of terms like "mean" and "significant". Their workaday role is to raise and address questions, asked "in the stream of life", about items whose appropriateness to Life the questioner is failing to discern. But construed as a question about the phenomenon of meaning – about appropriateness to Life – it becomes a peculiar one. "Why is anything appropriate to Life?" is no different from the question "Why is there Life?" – for Life (forms of life, the "human world") just is the arena or terrain of appropriateness, of the practices, engagements and purposes of creatures for whom, as Heidegger might put it, the appropriateness of any item is always an actual or potential issue. Certainly the question often raised by the naturalistically minded, concerning the role of meaning in the evolution of human beings from "mere" or "first" nature to culture or "second" nature, is poorly posed. For what is not even notionally separable from human Life cannot have played an evolutionary role in its emergence.

Finally, the import of meaning – what it "shows" – cannot be this or that particular dimension of Life. What the phenomenon of meaning shows is not that we humans are, in addition to whatever else we are, thus-and-so, but simply that we are humans – creatures possessed of Life or, better perhaps, ones whose mode of being is Life. That we produce meaningful items, from words and gestures to hammers and sonatas, and that we can discern and enquire into the significance of just about anything are not bolt-on extras, things we happen to do in addition to the rest of Life. Rather, to recall Merleau-Ponty's words, to be a participant in Life *is* to be an inveterate trafficker in meaning, to be "condemned" to it.

3 Language

Chapter 2 provided an informal survey of the reach of meaning, with attention drawn to the many fields to which meaningful items belong, the various focuses under which such items are put and the different frames employed for indicating the meanings of items. It did not, I urged, follow from the protean reach of meaning that "mean" and related terms were ambiguous. Nor, I argued, was it legitimate to expel any of our talk of meaning – for example, of "natural" meaning – from the purview of an account of the meaning of meaning. What the reach of meaning reflects, rather, is variety in what count as explanations of meaning. To amend Wittgenstein's remark on the concept of understanding, we should regard the various kinds of meaning explanations as going to "make up our concept of meaning" (1969: §532). Meaning is what explanations of meaning, deployed "in the stream of life", explain. These explanations, I suggested, indicate – in a manner that typically relies on background, implicit understanding – connection to Life. That connection I dubbed "appropriateness". My talk of Life and appropriateness was, of course, bland, but not empty, for it suggests a direction to be taken by enquiries into whatever fields of meaning engage our interest. Enquiry should focus on explanations of meaning in that field, in particular on the ways they serve to indicate the appropriateness of items in relation to Life.

In this chapter, I consider what, for many, is evidently the field most deserving of philosophical attention – that of linguistic items, pre-eminently the words, sentences and utterances of these that belong to or utilize natural languages, like English.

Assertion and system

Several reasons might be given for a concentration on linguistic meaning, most obviously the fact that natural languages have become our paramount vehicles of communication. Had history gone differently, picturing, gesturing or an extension of animal signalling might have been our primary means of communication. As it is, speaking the words of natural languages is the primary and remarkably versatile means. It might be argued, moreover, that it is no merely contingent matter that natural languages, rather than other "semiological systems", are primary. As Roland Barthes puts it, "objects, images and patterns of behaviour can signify, and do so on a large scale, but never autonomously; every semiological system has its linguistic admixture" (1968: 10). His point is that, to become an "extensive *system* of signs", the use of images, objects and gestures is parasitic on a linguistic ordering and representation of the world. Only language-users could become film-makers, say, or mimes. Barthes goes on to make a further, more contentious, claim: "it . . . [is] difficult to conceive of a system of images and objects whose *signifieds* can exist independently of language . . . [for] the world of signifieds is none other than that of language" (*ibid.*). This, in effect, is the thesis of "linguistic idealism", on which what words and other signs stand for – "signifieds" – could not exist in the absence of language. Language would then indeed be pre-eminent: not only other forms of communication, but the very world about which we communicate, are dependent upon it.

I do not pursue that contentious claim here (but see Chapter 4), since my present concern is not with the pre-eminence of language, but the pre-eminence or otherwise of certain ways of indicating or explaining the meaning of linguistic items, and hence with the centrality or otherwise of a type of meaning they have.

The literature is full of pronouncements of the form "The meaning of a sentence/word/utterance is . . .". Sometimes, such pronouncements are Theoretical: meanings are entities, specified in such pronouncements, which are postulated to play an explanatory role in a Theory of, say, linguistic behaviour. So taken, the pronouncements are, for reasons already given, of no interest to me. Nor are they of interest if read as insisting, absurdly, that only one sort of thing can count as explaining the meaning of a sentence, word or utterance. The charitable way to construe such pronouncements is as claiming that a certain way of indicating or explaining the meanings of linguistic items is especially central. They are pronouncements to the effect that there is a pre-eminent, central relationship of appropriateness that linguistic items – and perhaps only these – have to Life.

I shall suggest, unadventurously, that there are salient aspects of language which indeed guarantee that certain modes of meaning-explanation, less germane outside the linguistic field, indeed have their rightful place. More contentiously, I shall then argue that it is wrong to inflate the importance of that place in the manner done by many philosophers of language. Even charitably interpreted, pronouncements of the kind "The meaning of a sentence is . . ." are one-sided: there is no pre-eminent appropriateness, possessed by linguistic items, to be thus specified. It is not only "poets and preachers, writers and scholars" for whom words are among "the greatest riches of this earthly life" (Blair 1996: 150). Language and its deployments are indeed immensely rich, and it would be a symptom, to cite Paul Feyerabend's (2000) phrase, of a depressing "conquest of abundance" to try to contain within a formula the ways in which they are appropriate to Life.

There are two salient aspects in particular of natural languages to which, reasonably enough, philosophers have held that an account of linguistic meaning should be responsive. The first is that, while language may be put to many uses – commanding, questioning, warning, encouraging and so on – an obviously important and pervasive one is that of asserting or stating, of saying how things are. (Contrast gestures, which are more typically employed in such tasks as greeting and insulting than in conveying information.) The second aspect is that of systematicity. What a sentence is used to assert is often something we are able to work out from its constituent words and its syntactical organization. Sentences, moreover, stand to one another in the relations studied by logic – entailment, contradiction and so on. (Contrast gestures, once more, which are typically "simple" – without internal constituents and organization. While, moreover, it would be odd for someone to stick his tongue out at you when warmly shaking your hand, there is no logical contradiction between the two gestures.) Again, linguists inspired by Saussure (1966: Ch. 4) are able, with some success, to partition the lexicon of a language into "fields", within which there obtain relatively systematic relations of "association" and "opposition" among the terms.

Concentration on these two aspects of language has inspired the accounts of meaning that, at least among Anglo-American philosophers, have held centre stage in recent times. On those accounts, the pre-eminent use of language to make assertions implies that a central role in an account of meaning is played by the notion of *truth* – an account that must also incorporate appreciation of the systematic character of language when so deployed. It is not denied, of course, that language is put to other uses – imperatival and interrogative ones, for example – or that speakers can warn, promise and intimate as well as state or assert. But a common line is that such uses are catered for by extending or supplementing an account that takes as basic the informative, statemental function of sentences. The point may be put like this: we get our grip on the notion of meaning by focusing on what is asserted by declarative sentences, for this gives us their propositional content. With the idea of propositional content in place, we may then extend our grip by introducing the different "forces" – imperatival, interrogative and so on – with which propositions may be "presented" by speakers. To understand, say, the question "Is the sun round?", one must, therefore, already understand the proposition expressed by assertions of "The sun is round". After all, the answer "Yes" would be taken as an assertion of just that proposition.

Before I elaborate on the accounts of meaning I have in mind, I want to mention and, for the time being, sidestep an issue that has occupied much recent discussion. It is often urged that there is a conflict, a "Homeric struggle" (Strawson 1996: 105), between those accounts on which the notion of truth is the "key" to linguistic meaning and ones which emphasize the communicative intentions of speakers. The struggle, to recall some earlier terminology, is between accounts which respectively prioritize meaning-indicating frames like "This sentence means that p" and ones like "By uttering S, the speaker meant to V". Doubtless there are some real issues in the offing here, concerning the relation between a sentence's meaning and what speakers mean by uttering it. Can one, for example, identify the former with what speakers standardly mean when uttering it? But I mainly postpone such issues until Chapter 4, for they need not overly intrude into this one.

This is because it is perfectly possible for someone who finds the "key" to meaning in communicative intentions to hold that the pre-eminent intentions on which to focus are those of asserting that something is the case. The centrality of truth to the notion of meaning is, therefore, something that he too can maintain.

The simplest truth-centred account of meaning is one bequeathed by Frege (see, e.g., 1967: 89ff.). The meaning or sense of a word (or other sub-sentential constituent) is its "contribution" to the meanings of sentences in which it occurs, while the meaning of a sentence is given by indicating the conditions under which "it stands for the True" – its truth-conditions, those under which it would be true. An alternative account, inspired by epistemological considerations that need not detain us at present, is heir to the verificationism of the logical positivists. On this approach, understanding a sentence's meaning is not a matter of grasping the conditions under which it is true, but of recognizing what evidential conditions would justify or warrant one in asserting it to be true – its assertibility-conditions (see, e.g., Dummett 1976). On a third truth-centred approach, so-called "inferential role" semantics, what fixes the meanings of sentences is the latter's place within "practices of giving and asking for *reasons*". The person who understands "That's red", unlike the parrot who squawks it, knows what it does and doesn't follow from, and what it does and doesn't entail (Brandom 1994: 89). Understanding a sentence's meaning, therefore, is not a simple matter of knowing its truth-conditions; it requires, too, a grasp of what other truths would entail, and be entailed by, its truth.

This third approach illustrates how systematicity is also accommodated: to understand a sentence or word is necessarily to understand a large number of others to which they are inferentially related. "Grasping a concept involves mastering . . . inferential moves that connect it to many other concepts" (Brandom 1994: 89). But even the barer truth-conditions account invokes system. Champions of that account, like Davidson, argue that it is only when sentence-meanings are understood in terms of truth-conditions that precision is lent to Frege's insight that the meanings of words are their systematic contribution to those of sentences. What that identification facilitates, in effect, is a revamping of Tarski's "semantic theory of truth" as a theory of meaning. What Tarski (1956: Ch. VIII) showed was how to derive the truth-conditions of sentences of certain formal languages from rules governing their constituents. (For example, the rule governing "~" entails that "~P" is true just when "P" is false.) Suitably amended for natural languages, the Tarskian approach holds out the promise of *explaining* the systematic way that words contribute to the meanings of, say, English sentences, once these are identified in terms of truth-conditions.

A further reason is often urged for connecting truth and system. Consider the following problem for the unelaborated claim that to understand a sentence's meaning is to know the conditions under which it is true. I may know, since German friends reliably inform me, that a certain German sentence is true just in case snow is white. But that could not guarantee my understanding the sentence: for all I know it may mean the same as "Snow is white", "The stuff people ski on is white", or "Snow is the same colour as your pillow-case". My problem, in effect, is that I don't know *why* snow's being white makes the German sentence true. Only when I appreciate that this is solely because of the sentence itself – its constituents and organization – and not, in addition, because of extra-linguistic facts about skiing or pillow-cases, could I claim to know that it means the same as "Snow is white". For those alert to such problems, to understand a sentence's meaning is not, therefore, simply to know that it is true when . . ., but to know this solely on the basis of the sentence's structure and constituents. That latter knowledge, however, requires a grasp of the systematic contributions to sentences of particular constituents. Davidson's claim that "we can give the meaning of any sentence (or word) only by giving the meaning of every sentence (or word) in the language" (1984: 22) may be wildly exaggerated. But it dramatizes the point that we must be familiar with a generous slice of a language if we are to grasp the systematic contributions made by words to sentences, and hence to grasp whether a sentence's being true under certain conditions is due solely to its composition – and hence whether those conditions might plausibly be held to constitute its meaning.

Meaning and truth-conditions: the "quick" argument
I shall return later to the considerations, sketched above, that have inspired truth-centred accounts of meaning. First, I want to discuss

and reject a very quick argument for understanding the meaning of at least very many declarative sentences in terms of truth-conditions. This is an argument that seems to have convinced many writers – indeed, to have persuaded them that the equation is obvious.

The "very many" sentences to which the argument, in the first instance, applies are "context-free" sentences – those whose truth or falsity is not affected by such contextual factors as who utters them, when or where. "Snow is white" is context-free in this sense, while "I am sober today" is not. Once the equation of meanings and certain truth-conditions is established for context-free sentences, it can be extended and amended – so the hope goes – to cater for context-bound ones.

The "quick" argument goes like this. The following statement is evidently true:

"'Snow is white' is true if and only if snow is white"

Now replace the words "is true if and only if" by "means that". The result? Another evidently true statement:

"'Snow is white' means that snow is white"

Quite generally, there is a necessary equivalence between "S is true if and only if p" and "S means that p" when, in both cases, "p" is *the very same* (context-free) sentence as the one named by "S". Now surely, the argument goes, truly stating that S means that p is nothing less than to state S's meaning. What else or more could "Snow is white" mean than that snow is white? But, since "p" is also used to state S's truth-conditions, it follows that to state those truth-conditions is, at the same stroke, to indicate its meaning. Given the equivalence of "S is true if and only if p" and "S means that p", we can equate such a statement of truth-conditions with one of meaning. To know what "Snow is white" means – namely that snow is white – is nothing other than knowing what makes it true.

My problems with this argument concern the formula "S means that p", where, as stipulated, "p" is the very same sentence as that referred to by "S". Unlike, it would seem, those who deploy the argument, I have trouble understanding what "'Snow is white' means that snow is white" is saying. One is told often enough what it is *not* saying. It is not saying that "Snow is white" means (the same as) "Snow is white", for this would be to say something entirely trivial which someone could understand who has no idea what "Snow is white" means. (Even anglophone monoglots know that "Schnee ist weiss" means (the same as) "Schnee ist weiss".) In "S means that p", it is insisted, "p" is being *used* – to state a meaning – not merely "mentioned". But this is insufficient to dispel my worries. (For some related worries, see Rundle 1979.)

To begin with, one wonders when a statement of that form could be used, "in the stream of life", to explain to someone anything about a sentence's meaning. It is, one reads, "undeniable" that "'Snow is white' means that snow is white" "gives the meaning" of the sentence (Evans and McDowell 1976: viii). But most people, I suspect, *would* deny that one gives its meaning by saying, simply, that it means that snow is white – just as they would deny that one has given the location of a lost wallet by reporting that it is where it is. Of course, it is possible to imagine circumstances in which "S means that p" *might* serve in an explanation of meaning. Indeed, I imagined such circumstances on p. 29: "'Snow is white' means that snow is white. Period!" might inform someone that the sentence means just what it seems to, that it's not an idiom, say, or a hermetic message. But it is not such special uses of the formula that proponents of the "quick" argument have in mind. The onus is upon them, however, given its lack of a standard employment "in the stream of life", to explain the import of the formula.

One wonders, too, how objects – including sentences – can by themselves be used so as to indicate their own meanings. That old stone with "III" inscribed on it means that it's three miles to York: that it means this is not, however, something the stone by itself could serve to indicate. (The reason, incidentally, is *not* that this meaning can only be indicated by words: one can imagine silent strategies – involving, say, the use of a milometer – for conveying it.) It is no good pointing out that "'Snow is white' means that snow is white" is an instance of a very general frame, "S means that . . .", the vast majority of whose instances – for example, "'Snow is white' means that that stuff on the mountain top is white" – are unproblematic. The proper reply to this is that the usual intelligibility of "S means that . . ." does not extend to cases where the dots are replaced by the very sentence named by "S". Compare a logic student's reasonable worry that "A thing is identical with itself" – a "useless proposition", Wittgenstein remarks (1969: §216) – does not inherit the intelligibility of "A is identical with B", where "A" and "B" are different terms.

In the identity case, of course, the student's worry may be dispelled by telling him or her that, in logic, it is *stipulated* how identity statements, including "A is identical with A", are to be understood. Analogously, the onus is on those who place so much weight upon "S means that p" to stipulate how that formula is to be read (if not as a way of emphasizing that S is not an idiom or the like). Since they seem to find the formula transparent, however, this is not an obligation they tend to discharge. Nevertheless, it is not hard to discern the stipulative understanding that lurks in the background. "What we ought to be doing", when stating what sentences mean, is "stating something such that, if someone knew it, he would be able to speak and understand the language" (Evans and McDowell 1976: ix). The "we" here are, of course, "we Theorists", concerned with meanings in so far as these play a role in the explanation of linguistic ability. Indeed, one is explicitly informed a line later that statements of the form "S means that p" "provide a theoretical articulation of a speaker–hearer's competence".

What this amounts to is that "S means that p" is simply a Theorist's device for specifying what it is – *whatever* it is – that a competent speaker allegedly knows. "'Snow is white' means that snow is white" has no clear, pre-Theoretical sense, for its sense is only supplied through commandeering it for the statement of whatever it is that someone understands when he understands "Snow is white". Now there is nothing wrong *per se* with deciding to "represent" or "theoretically articulate" what speakers understand in the form "S means that p". But nothing whatsoever follows as to *what it is* that is understood by someone who knows the meaning of a sentence, for we have been given by the Theoretician no more than formulas, like "'Snow is white' means that snow is white", for labelling what is understood. In particular, it cannot follow that to understand a sentence is to know its truth-conditions. That would only follow if, on independent grounds, there were good reason to regard a grasp of truth-conditions as central to understanding meanings. The "quick" argument is, therefore, spurious, for it relied on there being a clear, pre-Theoretical content to "S means that p", one that could quickly be equated with that of "S is true if and only if p". But there is no such content, and nothing in the stipulated interpretation foisted upon the formula by "we Theorists" warrants a privileged connection between meaning and truth.

This result should not be surprising. It would surely have been magical if reflection on so peculiar a sentence as "'Snow is white' means that snow is white" could produce, like a rabbit from a hat, a substantive account of the meaning of meaning. So let us return to the less prestidigitative approaches of the previous section.

Words and sentences

The first thing to say about those approaches – which identified sentence-meanings with certain truth-conditions, assertibility-conditions and inferential roles respectively – is that, despite the usual perception, they should not be presented as rivals. Telling someone the conditions under which a sentence is true, spelling out the conditions under which he would be entitled to assert it and explaining what other sentences entail and are entailed by it can all be ways of enabling him to understand the sentence. Each, in its own fashion, can indicate when and why it is appropriate to assert the sentence. (In what follows, I generally refer only to the truth-conditions approach: my remarks can be amended to apply to the two other approaches.)

Secondly, even when attention is restricted to assertoric sentences, any number of further styles of indication count, in suitable contexts and on suitable occasions, as explaining a sentence's meaning to someone.

> "S is a statement that, in our country, children learn to make when . . ."
> "Here, we say S when we want to express . . ."
> "S is something it would be impolite to say when . . ."
> "S means almost the same as S*, but it would be more natural to say the former when . . ."

These are just a few of the styles, different from those privileged by the truth-centred approaches, in which meanings are explained, in which appropriateness is indicated. Or consider Wittgenstein's important point:

> We speak of understanding a sentence in the sense in which it can be replaced by another which says the same, but also in the sense in which it cannot be replaced by any other. (Any more than one musical theme can be replaced by another.)
>
> (1969: §531)

Since it is generally possible for a sentence to be "replaced" by one that shares its truth-conditions, it follows that explaining its meaning in terms of those conditions is not to explain it "in the sense in which it *cannot* be replaced by another". A whole dimension of linguistic appropriateness, therefore, is ignored if meaning-explanations are confined to those favoured by truth-centred accounts.

How, then, should we respond to the arguments adumbrated earlier for assigning truth a pre-eminent role in illuminating the meaning of meaning? The two main arguments were that assertion was the central function of language, and that only a truth-centred approach explains the systematic contribution to sentence-meanings in terms of which the meanings of words must be understood. Let's begin by examining that second argument.

Clearly its force will evaporate unless understanding words *is* a matter of recognizing their systematic contributions to the meanings of sentences. If this is not accepted, then what truth-centred approaches purport to explain is a will-o'-the-wisp. So let's ask why so many philosophers and linguists share this "contributivist" conviction. Their conviction rests, I suggest, on two claims, harmless in themselves, but prone to inflation. (What follows is indebted to Baker and Hacker 1980: Ch. VIII.) The first is the Fregean dictum that "only in a sentence have ... words really a meaning". We cannot, Frege insists, ask for the meaning of a word "in isolation, but only in the context of a sentence" (1959: x and §60). The second claim is that our understanding of sentences relies on antecedent understanding of component words; otherwise we should have to learn from scratch the meaning of each sentence that is new to us. These two claims might seem to be at odds: the first holding that to understand words, we must understand sentences; the second holding that to understand sentences, we must understand words.

But they are easily combined: to understand a new sentence, we must indeed already understand the component words; but to understand *them* is to have grasped, through past linguistic experience, their use in the context of sentences – a grasp then extended to the new sentence in question.

Soberly construed, the first claim simply adverts to the truth that it is only whole sentences that serve to communicate, say anything, or perform "speech acts". Counter-examples to this may either be cheerfully accepted as exceptions which prove the rule (e.g. "Hurrah!", "Ouch!") or be rejected as illegitimate ("Yes", by itself, is really a one-word *sentence*, as are any number of other single words uttered in response to questions). This uncontentious truth implies that someone who cannot understand sentences cannot, therefore, use words to say anything – a disability that amounts to not understanding the words at all. Soberly construed, the second claim simply reminds us that understanding sentences usually presupposes understanding the component words. (Only usually: understanding an idiomatic utterance, like "He kicked the bucket", does not require – and is not guaranteed by – knowing what "kick" and "bucket" ordinarily mean.)

The two claims, so construed, provide no warrant for holding that words systematically determine the meanings of sentences, and that they themselves have meaning only in virtue of this. To reach those conclusions, one must accept a hypothesis that, while often presented as a construal of the two claims, in fact belongs to a theoretical attempt to *explain* them – to explain, in effect, why words have meaning only within the context of sentences and how we understand new sentences. The idea is that the meaning of a word is a rule governing the effect on sentences' meanings of occurrences of the word within them. That explains why it is only in the context of sentences that the words have meanings, and how it is that we understand new sentences: we combine already acquired rules and apply them to previously unencountered strings of words. To take a favourite example, if the meaning of the logical connective "&" is specified by the rule

"P & Q" is true iff "P" is true and "Q" is true,

that shows why "&" has meaning only in the context of sentences and how – given the rules governing other connectives – we can work out the meaning of a sentence new to us, such as "(P ∨ Q) & ~R".

There is nothing wrong with sometimes invoking that style of explanation: the meanings of some symbols or words may legitimately be thought of as rules determining their contributions to sentences. But is there any reason to suppose that this is the standard, let alone uniquely legitimate, style? Indeed, do the phenomena of words' having meaning in the context of sentences and of the ability to understand new sentences call for explanation at all? At one level, they are "explained" simply by reiterating the two sober construals: one does not understand words unless one can use them to communicate, which requires employing them in sentences; and one understands new sentences through understanding their component words. There is, so to speak, nothing *deep* here that invites further explanation. That we can understand sentences which are new to us – that our understanding is, as Chomsky (1968) peculiarly calls it, "creative" – is often taken to be some extraordinary accomplishment that cries out for theoretical explanation. It is hard to see why. After all, "creative" understanding is hardly peculiar to linguistic knowledge. Indeed, it is difficult to think of any intelligent activities where we would credit people with practical understanding unless they could exercise it on occasions which differ from those on which they acquired it. Someone does not understand how to boil an egg if at a loss what to do when the saucepan is a different colour from the one his mother used when teaching him. Equally, his failure to understand a generous number of new sentences containing the word "egg" is a good reason for doubting that he does, after all, understand that word. There are not two capacities – understanding words and understanding sentences – linked by some obscure mechanism of rules that the theorist uncovers. Rather, to understand sentences – old and new – is *criterial* for understanding words.

Even if the two sober claims did call for "deep" explanation, it would be wrong to provide one in the form of the general hypothesis that word-meanings are rules that systematically determine the meanings of sentences, their truth-conditions, say. The meanings of our ordinary descriptive terms are nothing of the sort. To understand these terms and to explain to people what they mean cannot be a matter of grasping and indicating such rules, for there aren't any. This can be seen by reflecting that a word, without being ambiguous, typically contributes in any number of quite different ways, not subsumable under some rule, to what is asserted by sentences containing it. Consider, for example, the word "green" and its contribution to sentences like "Those leaves are green". That sentence is not ambiguous, despite its availability to communicate a range of very different circumstances, to say something true under very different, sometimes incompatible, conditions. It may be used to convey, *inter alia*, that the leaves look green under normal conditions; that the leaves have been sprayed with green paint; that, although they don't look green – having been sprayed red – they are naturally green; or that they have been painted, as by a pointillist, with yellow and blue dots, so as to look green from a distance. The "*inter alia*" is important here, for there is no principled way of determining in advance the range of circumstances that we would recognize "Those leaves are green" as truly reporting. That is a good reason for denying that the sentence, simply because it is available for reporting such different circumstances, is therefore ambiguous: there could be no hope of ever specifying its different meanings, and the idea of unknown meanings is an unattractive one. (If the sentence is ambiguous, it is for other reasons, such as its availability to state that the leaves are eco-friendly or, more eccentrically, that they are inexperienced or envious.)

Charles Travis, to whom I owe both the example and the line of argument, spells out their implication for word-meanings: "any . . . expression may, *meaning what it does*, make any number of different contributions to truth conditions of wholes in which it figures" (1997: 87, my italics). To understand a word like "green" cannot consist in grasping a rule that dictates its systematic contribution to the truth-conditions of sentences containing it – for there is no such contribution. Rather, to understand it, and to be able to explain its meaning in the different contexts in which it is used, is to possess a capacity to recognize the appropriateness of the word's use within sentences – in any number of contexts – for communicating what speakers aim, according to context, to communicate. That capacity is not to be represented as the grasp of some rule, for as Travis remarks, "a *rule* is no substitute for [the] sensitivity to surroundings" essential to recognizing the appropriateness of using *these* words to communicate *that* situation (1994: 183). A rule, however complicated, could never substitute for this, for, as Derrida expresses it, the "infinitely new contexts" in which a word's use may be recognized as appropriate are "nonsaturable" (1982: 320). There is no possibility, that is, of mopping up this infinity of contexts into a formula that articulates and represents our understanding of "green" – or of "dog", "leaf", "cup" and most other words in our lexicon.

I return in the final section to the picture of the understanding of linguistic meaning which is being rejected here. What I have argued in this section is that one of the main arguments for prioritizing truth in an account of the meaning of meaning is a bad one. According to that argument, only truth-centred accounts can properly explain the systematic contribution of word-meanings to sentence-meanings. Since there is, in the case of most words, no such systematic contribution to explain, the argument dangles.

Truth and relevance

The other main argument for prioritizing truth rested on the alleged pre-eminence, among the many uses of language, of its assertoric or truth-stating function. It's not transparent, however, what this pre-eminence is supposed to consist in, nor why, precisely, it should privilege indications of meaning in terms of truth-conditions. Presumably, the pre-eminence is not a statistical one, for even if statements outnumber other speech acts, the relevance of this is opaque. Nor, I think, is it some sort of practical pre-eminence, to do with the contribution of assertoric discourse to human progress or civilization, that is intended.

On p. 43, we briefly encountered one consideration in support of the pre-eminence of the statemental. According to this, the understanding of questions, commands and the like is parasitic on that of suitably related statements. To know what "Shut the door!" means, I must know what "The door is shut" means. It is, the thought continues, through attending to assertions that we come by the notion of a proposition, of the content of an utterance. Now since "The door is shut", "Is the door shut?" and "Shut the door!" are related through "presenting" a single proposition, but in different "moods", it follows that understanding of questions and commands derives from that of statements.

This argument for the pre-eminence of the statemental is unpersuasive, however. To begin with, the idea that a statement is related to a corresponding question and command *because* they share a common proposition sounds like a reificationist myth. "Is the door shut?" is related to "The door is shut" in that the former asks a question to which the latter is an answer. There is no call to introduce some common soil, a proposition, in which the two are rooted. So we are left with the insistence that understanding of commands and so on is parasitic on that of assertions. The difficulty is then to see why this dependence is not symmetrical. Would we credit someone with understanding "The door is shut" who was incapable of asking if the door is shut, telling someone to shut it, and much else – warning that the door is shut, promising to shut it, idly contemplating whether it is shut and so on? After all, we judge a person's competence in a language not on the basis of a contextless blurting out of statements, impeccably true as they may be, but on that of the appropriateness of his statements, not only to extra-linguistic situations, but to discursive context. Typically, it is in the flow of conversation – where questions are raised, instructions given, guarantees sought, warnings issued, speculations mooted – that statements are judged (in)appropriate and speakers (in)competent. To hang the matter of people's linguistic understanding on their understanding of statements isolated from these conversational flows is arbitrary.

But are we not ignoring an argument for privileging truth-stating that has, it seems, convinced many people of the centrality of truth in the understanding of linguistic meaning? We need to ask, so the argument goes, how people manage to communicate at all – to convey information, issue warnings, make enquiries or whatever. This is to ask, in part, what it is for them to share a language. The answer to that question cannot be, simply, that they make the same sorts of noises: it is crucial, obviously, that the noises have a similar significance for them. A language, the idea goes, may be thought of as a *pairing* of linguistic items (sequences of phonemes, say) with something else. In the case of sentences, the pairing is with truth-conditions. Speakers share a language, it is argued, just in case they mutually conform to a certain "convention" – that of uttering sentences of that language just in case they believe them to be true; believe, that is, that the truth-conditions with which the sentences are paired actually obtain. It is in virtue of conforming to this "convention of truthfulness" (Lewis 1969: 177ff.) that speakers share a language and so manage to communicate effectively with one another. Only when we recognize others as trying to speak the same truths by sentences that we try to speak by them do we recognize them as communicating in our language. So truth-stating is indeed the privileged deployment of language, the *sine qua non* of there being a shared language to deploy.

The objection to this is simple: there is no convention of truthfulness conformed to by speakers of a language, no general presumption that indicative sentences are put forward as true. The objection is not that speakers often deceive and that all of us know this: as Kant saw, lying and deception presuppose a general presumption of honesty. Rather, the objection is that a great deal of our talk, while not dishonest, is neither intended nor received as truth-stating (see Cooper 1997). To begin with, much of our talk is, in a broad sense, figurative. Apart from metaphorical and ironic talk, consider, for example, the extent to which we engage in harmless, everyday hyperbole. There weren't two hundred people at the party, but "thousands"; it wasn't just very difficult for me to leave the party, but "absolutely impossible"; it wasn't just an unenjoyable party, but a "nightmare". Next, much of our talk is "ritualistic". "I'm fine, thanks", said in reply to "How are you?"; "That was a lovely evening", said on leaving the party; "It's tragic", said on hearing of someone's death – these are utterances into whose truth only the naïve or unskilled interlocutor enquires. Again, many statements, without being ritualistic, are produced for social and other purposes – breaking an awkward silence, comforting someone in distress, playing devil's advocate – that render the speaker's commitment to their truth a matter of secondary interest at most. Finally, a particularly pervasive phenomenon that tells against any general presumption of truthfulness is that of so-called "loose talk" (Sperber and Wilson 1986: 233ff.). If, in the context of everyday enquiries, someone tells me it's 3pm, when it's actually 2.59, or that he has been to Paris dozens of time, when he's only been twenty-three times, I don't regard him as having flouted a convention.

One might seek to preserve a convention of truthfulness in the following manner (see Grice 1989: Ch. 2). While there is, for the reasons just given, only a weak, easily defeasible presumption that what people actually *say* is intended to be true, there is a strong presumption that they intend to *convey* (or "implicate") something true. "It's 3pm" is false, but what the speaker intended to convey – that it's around 3pm – is true. "There were thousands of people there" is false, but truly conveys that the party was crowded. The idea is that, when the weak presumption of a statement's truth is defeated, the audience – which assumes the speaker is a responsible conversationalist – searches round for a truth that he is trying to convey. Provided this can successfully be done, no flouting of the (amended) convention of truthfulness has occurred.

Part of my response to this manoeuvre is postponed until the following section. For the moment, I simply remark that, as a way of dealing with at least some of the recalcitrant cases listed two paragraphs earlier, it is unpromising. The idea, for example, that someone speaking metaphorically or ironically is generally trying to convey some true proposition, distinct from what he actually stated, is a poor one. It may work for hackneyed metaphors, like "Your wife is an angel", but not for fresh or "creative" ones, like "Architecture is frozen music" – whose effect is not to convey some particular proposition, but to provoke a novel perspective or line of thought. (More on this in Chapter 6.) Again, the conversationalist who plays devil's advocate, or simply "tries out" some ideas in a "brain-storming" session, does not intend to convey, any more than explicitly to state, some true proposition.

If there is some general presumption or convention at work, it is not that speakers try to state or convey truth, but that they say "something worth attending to" (Culler 1983: 113). Or, as Sperber and Wilson (1986) have vigorously argued, that speakers endeavour to say things that are "relevant". In some contexts, of course, a person will only say or convey something relevant or worth attending to if it is *true*: but that's just one, context-relative way in which relevance is assured. Such a conclusion pleasingly chimes with my remarks, in Chapter 2, on meaning and appropriateness, for it supports the thoughts that in understanding one another's words, we are identifying their appropriateness, and that to explain what their words mean is to indicate their appropriateness. Really, it should be unsurprising if the general character of meaning-explanations – indication of appropriateness to Life – should belong, in particular, to explanations of linguistic meaning. Language is not some extra, isolatable dimension of Life, but the medium in which much of it is conducted. It is in and through speech that a multitude of the purposive activities that belong to Life are pursued and prosecuted. One could hardly expect, then, that speech should be subject to much less than the full range of appraisals of appropriateness and relevance to Life that our wider activities are.

In usual explanations of linguistic meaning, as in those of non-linguistic meaning, Life is, of course, in the background. One does not need to lay bare a whole culture to see how "It's 3pm" and "The party was a nightmare" may be appropriate utterances. The indispensability of that background becomes evident, however, when we reflect on the difficulty of understanding speakers whose Life is not ours. For what we then lack is precisely that shared sense of appropriateness essential to understanding their utterances. "Left out, cut off, isolated", as at an African cattle market or Japanese tea ceremony, we are "not able to understand" what is being communicated (Friggieri 1991, as elaborated in Serracino Inglott 1995: 2f.). Consider, in particular, our inability to do something that we do all the time when "at home": to recognize what, beyond anything explicitly spoken, speakers are communicating. If you tell me that someone greeted you in the street, I take it for granted that the person did not do so in a Sherman tank or in the shape of a dog, though your words do not explicitly exclude such possibilities. That is because I take you to share my sense of appropriateness – one that would have been violated by your failure to remark on something so salient and untoward as someone coming up to you in a tank or incarnated as a dog. With such a shared sense suspended – as it is when we are not "at home", when we are among people whose Life is not ours – we do not know what is deemed salient or mundane, striking or inconspicuous. We do not, that is, know what "they" find it appropriate to remark upon, and hence are not in our domestic situation of being able to grasp what situations their words communicate.

So the attempt to prioritize meaning-explanations that indicate the truth- or assertibility-conditions of sentences fails. Such indications must take their unprivileged place alongside the many other ways in which the appropriateness of speech to Life are indicated. It is not a convention of truthfulness, but a shared sense of appropriateness, that enables communication and the speaking of a common language.

Robotics

At the risk of some repetition, in this final section I highlight a merit, as it seems to me, of the approach to linguistic meaning that, in opposition to truth-centred accounts, I have followed. Those accounts are only the most heavily subscribed versions of a wider, "purist" conception of meaning, and it is the implausibility of the latter that my discussion has prepared us to recognize.

For purists, my criticisms of truth-centred accounts are guilty of contaminating semantic issues with pragmatic considerations. Certainly, my rejection of two theses – those of word-meanings as systematic contributions to sentences and of the pre-eminence of the statemental – relied on attending to language as it is used in context, "in the stream of life". For purists, linguistic competence is a dog-legged affair. It comprises, first, knowledge of a set of semantic rules that determine the contribution of words to the meanings of sentences, conceived of as conditions (such as truth-conditions) or entities (propositions, possible worlds or whatever) with which the sentences are paired. Competence requires, secondly, the grasp of pragmatic rules – a "convention of truthfulness", "conversational maxims", a "principle of relevance" or whatever – that determine the interpretation of the utterance, on any occasion, of a sentence whose meaning has been fixed by the semantic rules. It is granted that "The leaves are green", "It's 3pm", "There were thousands of people at the party", or "Architecture is frozen music" are available appropriately to communicate something not settled by semantics. The slack, it is argued, is taken up by pragmatic principles that enable deduction of what is communicated.

Purism in effect advocates what another of its critics has called "a way of conceiving meaning as purified of the various formations of culture and of the human form of life" (Mulhall 2001: 149). Culture and Life enter in only after the bend in the dog-leg – at the pragmatic level. (In another, Saussurean, idiom, they enter at the level of *parole*, not *langue*.) Some of my misgivings with purism – for example, its unpromising treatment of figurative talk – have already been mooted. Here I add two further objections.

To pick up on a point stressed in Chapter 2, even if one is sympathetic to the dog-legged picture, there is no good reason to restrict the notion of meaning to what is, allegedly, determined at the first, semantic stage. That would be a stipulation that flies in the face of our ordinary, catholic talk of meaning when, for example, we enquire about or explain what such-and-such words, sentences or utterances mean. It is, to take an example at random, perfectly natural for a character in a Chinese novel to wonder about "the precise meaning of the words" inscribed on a stone, "Be as bold as the rocks of Mount Tai" (Gao 2001: 91) – even though his puzzlement is not of a kind to be removed by semantic information. He knows perfectly well that the words exhort one to be as courageous as certain rocks. What he doesn't know is the meaning of that exhortation.

This objection will not, however, unduly disturb the purists. Granted, they will reply, that it may be cavalier to hijack the term "meaning" to refer to what is determined by semantic rules, the important thing is to appreciate that this – call it "semantic content", if you like – is settled independently and in advance of pragmatic, contextual considerations. Let's agree, for the sake of argument at least, that if the purist's picture is persuasive, then his niggardly, stipulative use of "meaning" is a forgivable peccadillo. But is it, to turn to my second objection, persuasive? In my judgement – like that of, *inter alia*, Wittgenstein, Heidegger, Merleau-Ponty and Stanley Cavell – the picture is a parody of linguistic mastery, one that portrays robotic, not human, communication. (Some of what follows owes to Stephen Mulhall's (2001: Part 1) elegant articulation of this point.)

One might imagine creatures who fit the purist conception and who, on a brief, superficial acquaintance, might be mistaken for ordinary speakers of at least some fragments of English. Wittgenstein invites us to imagine such cases with some of his "language games", whose point is to stress the difference between these and the full-blown use of language (see Cavell 1996). One thinks especially of the "game" in §1 of *Philosophical Investigations* where, to respond to a written request for five red apples, a "grocer" must consult rules for counting and matching names to colours. Perhaps we don't have to *imagine* such creatures, for some of us approximate to the purist picture when groping about in a foreign language: we *work out* the semantic content of the sentences from dictionaries and grammars and, where necessary, invoke what we have discovered about the natives' linguistic customs to ascertain what, on particular occasions, they are communicating by utterances of their sentences. Again, the purist picture may roughly fit the speech of some brain-damaged people and of Asperger-syndrome patients. Merleau-Ponty (1962: 196) discusses the case of a man who, while still able to speak, does so only "stereotypically" and by painstakingly preparing his sentences in advance, as if he were a virtual beginner in a foreign tongue.

Such cases, real or imaginary, have only to be described for the contrast with fully fledged mastery of one's language to become apparent. In those cases, the person's production of and responses to words have a robotic character: they are akin to the output of a computer programmed to churn out and process messages. Phenomenologically, the idea that, at all generally, we must, like the robot-men, consult rules in order to speak and understand is wildly implausible. For the most part, our mastery consists in the smooth, effortless, spontaneous ways we speak and recognize what other speakers are conveying. There is nothing, in particular, to be said for the idea that we are primed to hear sentences as communicating their semantic content, and then proceed to deploy pragmatic rules when we notice, in specific contexts, that something other than this is being communicated – as when, say, an utterance is too silly to take at face value.

The implausibility of supposing that, even when rules are available, we generally speak and interpret through "going by the rules" is not the only consideration. It should also be appreciated that our linguistic mastery is displayed by going beyond whatever could be represented as accordance with rules. In Merleau-Ponty's striking figure, our language is "like a wave [that] gathers and poises itself to hurtle beyond its . . . limits" (1962: 197). His point invites comparison with one made by the poet George Seferis (1982: 61) when he speaks of a *tension* between meaning and language, between what "wants to be expressed" and what is needed to "give a form" to this. These two "forces" are "unified" in *style* – the style of speakers, partly shared and partly unique to each of them, that, in Merleau-Ponty's words, is the manner in which they "take up a position in the world of [their] meanings" (1962: 193). It would be wrong to think of this "style" – of "authentic", as against "ossified", "sedimented", stereotypical, speech – as some ornamental extra or the preserve of poets. It is the speech in which many of us engage day in day out: when we come out with the *mot juste*, or exploit the sound of a word in preferring it to some synonym, or recognize that, yes, that was just the way to put it, or rephrase and improvise on another's words, or extend a term's use in a novel context, or hit on an illuminating analogy for explaining an opaque emotion, or, in the sinuous flow of conversation, bend and adjust our words in response to those of our interlocutors – and so on and so on. "Rephrase", "improvise", "extend", "bend" – these are terms familiar from descriptions of players of jazz music. And, indeed, the master of his language, like the jazz player, does not rigidly read from a "score", from a rule-book. He is someone who improvises on, bends and extends the materials he has inherited.

Finally, it would be hopeless to represent the capacity to interpret utterances as knowledge of rules or principles that, supplementing those which determine semantic content and taking contextual features into account, determine interpretations. For the context in which interpretation proceeds is Life itself. Only against that total and unsurveyable backdrop do particular contextual features permit or dictate how someone's words are to be taken. Interpretation, as Derrida reminds us, is limited by context, but the context is limitless. To be "at home" in a culture is only in modest part to identify the rules and conventions to which its members conform. More centrally, it is to share with them a sense of what matters, a sense of what is relevant and appropriate to do and say, and that "suitable sensitivity" to surroundings of which I spoke earlier. When stripped of all of that, no amount of knowledge of contextual detail will enable one, with any confidence, to assume an understanding of what those who *are* at home in that culture convey and communicate.

Knowledge, meaning
4 **and world**

As in Chapter 3, the focus of the present one is linguistic meaning. However, the issues considered are not peculiar to that domain and it will sometimes be therapeutic to have reminders of this. It may be that certain views to be discussed sound rather less plausible when we recall that gestures and facial expressions, say, also have their meanings. The chapter covers a lot of ground, but the matters discussed are intimately related. To begin with, there is some unfinished business from Chapter 3. There we noted in passing a dispute as to whether understanding sentences has to do with grasping, not their truth-conditions, but those under which we are warranted in asserting them. We touched, as well, on a dispute as to whether speaker's meaning, rather than word- or sentence-meaning, is the more primitive notion. I shall return to those disputes, albeit briefly, in the context of considering issues – flagged in Chapter 1 – that may be subsumed under the heading of "knowledge and meaning". In Chapter 1, I remarked that an account of meaning, besides saying something about the import, function and status of meaning, should address philosophical issues that reflection on meaning is apt to spawn. ("Besides" is perhaps not the right word, since the hope is that an account of, say, the status of meaning – notably one in terms of appropriateness to Life – will contribute to resolving the issues.)

The issues gathered under the heading "knowledge and meaning" fall into two kinds. The first concern knowledge *of* meanings. How, if at all, do we know what items mean? Are there really facts about meanings for us to know? The second concern knowledge of the world. Do the "symbolic forms" through which we try to describe or otherwise represent the world serve as windows on to the world or as obstructive veils? Less figuratively, is the nature of our understanding of words and other meaningful items compatible with the idea that these articulate how the world anyway, objectively, is independently of that articulation? Put in current jargon, the issues to be discussed are those of "meaning-scepticism" and "anti-realism". They are not unrelated; indeed, I will be suggesting that the best response to meaning-scepticism invokes a perspective that is incompatible with a "realist" picture of a world independent of human "ways of meaning".

Scepticism

So-called meaning-scepticism might better be labelled "meaning-nihilism", for the point of authors associated with the position is not that there *are* meanings, about which we are unfortunately doomed to ignorance or, at best, to beliefs that fall short of knowledge. Their point, rather, is that there is nothing to know or hold reasonable beliefs about. Despite this, their strategy, in the first instance, is similar to that of older sceptics about, say, the possibility of scientific knowledge.

The strategy is this. Imagine ourselves in the "ideal" position of having established all the evidence, all the facts, that could possibly be established in support of the claim that a speaker or a word means such-and-such. Not even being in that position, it is argued, warrants our making that claim. This is because it is possible to imagine any number of rival claims as to what is meant, each as compatible with the established evidence and facts as the first claim. Since, *ex hypothesi*, *all* the relevant evidence is in, nothing can then turn up which would rationally motivate accepting any one claim rather than another.

A natural response to this argument is that it at most shows that we can't be sure what is meant, *not* that there was nothing meant at all by speaker or by word. But the sceptic's reasonable counter to this response is to deny any sense to the idea of meanings of which one could be forever, and necessarily, ignorant. Unlike, perhaps, the ultimate particles of matter, meanings – if there are any – could not be beyond our ken: meanings that could not be learnt, identified and explained would be nothing. If there is no possible way of telling what is meant, nothing *is* meant. This is why meaning-sceptics are nihilists – as the following well-known manifestos make clear: "The point is not that we cannot be sure" whether hypotheses about meanings are true, "but that there is not even . . . an objective matter to be right or wrong about" (Quine 1960: 73); "There can be no such thing as meaning anything by any word" (Kripke 1982: 55).

But why suppose that no amount of evidence could show that a speaker or a word meant this rather than that? "Well," say the sceptics, "consider anything that *might* be thought sufficient evidence and we will show you, in each case, that it is compatible with any number of rival meaning-hypotheses". Sceptics differ, however, over what they are willing to consider even as putative evidence. For Quine, "there is nothing in linguistic meaning beyond what is to be gleaned from overt behaviour in observable circumstances" (1996: 446). So if overt behaviour cannot determine meaning, nothing can. And it cannot. If, to take his famous example, the behaviour is consistent with translating a native expression, "gavagai", as "rabbit", so it is with translating the expression as, say, "instance of rabbithood", "undetached rabbit-parts", or "case of rabbiting". (It is, at any rate, if we provide correspondingly odd translations of other native expressions as well.) More generally, "rival systems" of translation can each "fit the totality of speech behaviour" equally well (1960: 72). Since, for Quine, there is nothing to the meanings of native expressions not capturable in translation, then if translation is indeterminate, so are these meanings. Hence, there are no such meanings. Since, moreover, each English speaker is, in effect, "translating" into his own idiolect the words of any other speaker of English – since "translation begins at home" – the conclusion is unaffected when we consider expressions in our home language. Nothing in your overt behaviour could show that by "rabbit" you mean to talk of rabbits rather than undetached rabbit-parts or whatever.

Others sympathetic to meaning-scepticism, such as Kripke and Derrida, are more generous than Quine in what they allow as putative evidence. Nor do their arguments go via the detour of translation. Kripke's meaning-sceptic, for example, argues as follows. Suppose that all the facts we have ascertained about a person – ones not restricted to "overt behaviour" – seem to establish that by "+" or "plus" he means the function of addition, that he is following a rule to the effect that "$x + y$", for any two numbers, refers to their sum. Now suppose that, tomorrow, he is asked what $68 + 57$ – numbers larger than those he has previously encountered – come to, and that he answers "5". We should naturally conclude that he has either misunderstood the question, made a mistake, or now means something different by "+". Indeed, we must so conclude in order to retain our belief about what, up until that point, he has meant by "+". The trouble is, Kripke argues, that all the evidence in support of that belief is consistent with supposing that, in answering "5", the person is *correctly* applying some *other* rule which he has *always* been following – such as "$x + y = y + x$, unless either x or y is greater than 57, in which case $x + y = 5$". Kripke's inspiration, here, is Wittgenstein's remark (1969: §201) that "every course of action can be made out to accord with the rule" – for one can adjust the rule for the action to fit it.

The general thought is this: whether we think of meaning something as following a rule, engaging in a practice, applying words in keeping with some custom or whatever, all the facts we can marshal for supposing that someone means such-and-such are ones about what he has done *so far*. The evidential base, therefore, is finite, limited. No such set of facts determines what he means, for they are not facts about what he will go on to do, which they would have to be to settle his meaning. *Whatever* he goes on to do – answering "5", calling men "women", denying that snow is white – can be made out to conform with *some* rules/practices/customs that we may imagine him to have been following, and hence to be consistent with his having meant things quite different from what we supposed. The facts we can marshal, therefore, do not constitute his meaning this rather than that. Hence there is no fact as to what he means.

Strong stuff, it seems – and all the stronger if, as several have argued, meaning-scepticism is bound to inflate into a wider, "global" scepticism. After all, if the truth of a statement is a function both of its meaning and how things stand in the world, won't indeterminacy of meaning entail indeterminacy of truth-value? (see Wright 1984). Indeed, will it make sense to speak of there being determinate facts of any kind? If all the evidence about a speaker's use of " + " is compatible with his meaning any number of different things by it, it would seem, by parallel reasoning, that all the evidence in support of the putative fact that there is a tree in the meadow would also be evidence for quite different facts – for example, that there is a tree there if observed before a certain time, otherwise there is a hippopotamus in the meadow (Stroud 1996: 319). If so, every observation we make can be made out to accord with "the facts" – a *reductio ad absurdum* of the notion of facts.

Mentalism

Even if meaning-scepticism does not inflate into "global" scepticism, it sounds startling enough for many philosophers to have striven either to refute it or to draw its sting. By this stage, some readers must be impatiently complaining that something crucial has so far been omitted – the mind. Let's grant, they say, that "overt behaviour" leaves meaning indeterminate. That just shows we are looking in the wrong place. Surely speakers themselves know what they mean, and this is because meaning something is a mental, psychological process. The failure of the relevant mental phenomena to be determinately manifest in behaviour doesn't entail that they are not there, or that they are unknowable, at least by the person to whose mind they belong.

Meaning-sceptics do not, however, *ignore* the mental. Rather, they *argue* that invoking it cannot secure determinacy of meaning. In arguing this, they are men of their times: a striking feature of twentieth-century discussion of meaning was widespread hostility to "mentalistic", "psychologistic" or "ideational" accounts that locate meanings "in the head". Before returning to meaning-scepticism, it will be useful to review that hostility. An often-told story is that, in the bad old days – of Locke and Condillac – meanings were treated as mental items ("ideas", "images") that words and other signs "stand for". The new era began with Frege's insistence that meanings, unlike such mental items, are not "subjective", but "common property", the objects of public, shared acquaintance. "The reference and sense of a sign", therefore, must be sharply "distinguished from the associated idea" (Frege 1966: 58–9). Whether or not they accept Frege's own "Platonic" conception of meanings as entities occupying a "third world" beyond the material and mental ones, few later philosophers have recommended a return to/the bad old days. (Among the few, as Roy Harris reminds us, are those MIT linguists for whom, in a suitably "hi-tech" revamping of "ideationism", meanings are "trapped inside the brain" (2002: 27).)

This is indeed more story than history. For one thing, it is almost certainly wrong to construe Locke's remark that "*words* . . . came to be made use of by men as the signs of their ideas" (1975: III.ii.1) as indicating commitment to a mentalistic "theory of meaning" (see Hacking 1975: Ch. 4). For another, there were thinkers before Frege – Nietzsche and Dilthey, for example – who rejected any picture of meanings as mental items associated with words and signs. More importantly, there are, one would hope, more than a "few" who would resist the triumphalist claim that specifications of meaning are *never* ones of what is "in the head (or, maybe, the heart)", that it is *always* a gross error so to locate a meaning. Meaning, we have seen, is what is indicated by explanations of meanings. Among such explanations, there are those which, quite unexceptionally, serve to indicate mental items, to exhibit the appropriateness of certain words to, say, an emotional state. ("What do you think all these expressions of affection in his letters mean?" – "That he's pining for you, of course".) We should note, as well, that even if it were always an error to identify a meaning with an "idea" or other mental item, this would not show, just like that, that it is wrong to invoke the mental in an attempt to block meaning-scepticism. Someone might argue that while *what* someone means is never to be identified with such an item, it is nevertheless something "in the head" which settles that this *is* what he meant.

Still, we should grant – in connection with the first point just made – that most explanations of meaning do not take the form of indicating, explicitly at least, anything "in the heads" of speakers. They may, for example, serve to indicate features of a word's use, or the conditions for applying it to things. Indeed, as we shall shortly see, there are good reasons for thinking that some explanations *cannot* be construed as indicating mental states, processes or occurrences, even covertly or implicitly. Those reasons are of a kind, moreover, which imply that it cannot be "mental facts" that generally constitute people's meaning what they do by their words. Hence, appeals to "the mind" will not serve to refute the meaning-sceptic. (Parenthetically, one wonders if "mentalism" would ever have attracted people had their focus been less exclusively upon linguistic meaning. The thought that, unusual contexts aside, the significance we seek in a ritual or a conventional gesture of greeting is something "trapped inside the mind" sounds distinctly uninviting. Words, perhaps because of "silent speech", can seem harder to prise away from what may be going on "inside". When I "hear-myself-speak", there seems to be an "absolute proximity . . . of voice . . . and meaning" (Derrida 1976: 12).)

Two good reasons for holding that, often at least, specifications of meanings could not be of anything "in the head" have been advanced by Hilary Putnam (1975). The first draws attention to such familiar facts as this: most English speakers are rightly credited with understanding the word "spaniel", even though rather few of them could picture a spaniel, tell you what it is other than "a sort of dog", pick spaniels out from other dogs and so on. This is possible, Putnam remarks, because of our acceptance of "a division of linguistic labour". Given that some people, "the experts", can distinguish spaniels, describe them and the like, the rest of us – provided we defer to them – enjoy a vicarious understanding of the word. As such, it need certainly not be something "in the head" – a spaniel-image, a spaniel-concept or whatever – that constitutes a person's meaning what he does by "spaniel": it is at most the experts whose heads are thus furnished.

Putnam's second argument is dramatized in his famous "twin-earth" thought-experiment. Imagine that there is no psychological difference at all between us and speakers on some other planet with respect to the word "dog". The "idea" they associate with it is the same as ours. But suppose the creatures they call "dogs" are, unknown to them or us, ones made in a laboratory, of synthetic flesh. In that case, says Putnam, their word "dog" does not mean what ours does: hence, meanings "ain't in the head", for there is no difference between our and the extraterrestrials' heads. Actually, Putnam's conclusion is too sweeping: given a certain focus on what the extraterrestrials mean, it could be perfectly in order to say that they mean what we mean by "dog", even though what they call dogs are machine-made. More generally, what people have in mind can, in appropriate contexts of enquiry, be germane to their meanings. If it were a central, salient and highly operative belief about dogs in some tribe that dogs were reincarnated criminals, it wouldn't be a *mistake* to include that in an indication of what their word for dogs means. Still, what Putnam's argument establishes is that, sometimes at least, meaning-indicators make essential mention of what words refer to *irrespective* of what the speakers may *think* about what is referred to. Sometimes, that is, our interest in a word's meaning is an "externalist" one, in the appropriateness it possesses in virtue of its "hook-up" or causal connections with the world.

Considerations like Putnam's – to recall a topic from Chapter 3 – are among those militating against the contention that speaker's meaning is "prior" to the meaning of words, sentences and other bearers of meaning. According to that contention, what a word means is a function of what individual speakers intend to communicate with its help. "Division of linguistic labour" cases are a stark reminder that speakers may mean by their words what exceeds their communicative intentions. The non-expert cannot, in his ignorance, intend to communicate everything that the man from Cruft's will understand when he informs the latter that the Joneses have just bought a spaniel. "Twin-earth" cases are a stark reminder that what speakers in different communities intend to communicate may be the same, while what they end up meaning – due to "external" factors – is different in the two cases. Doubtless, many other considerations conspire against the image of the individual speaker who, as Derrida ironically describes him, is "agent, author, and master" of the meanings he expresses (1981: 28). A person's language is too embroiled with the world and the lives of his fellows for him generally to determine, by himself, what he may be taken to say and mean. That's why, as Saussure remarked, "language is not a function of the speaking subject" (1966: 14).

Let's return to the meaning-sceptics, for their favourite objection to invocation of the mental in the attempt to secure meanings has yet to emerge. The objection is that invoking mental items for this purpose is useless, since scepticism about the meanings of words simply re-arises as scepticism about these mental items. These cannot decide between rival construals of word-meanings, since they themselves are open to rival construals. This was Wittgenstein's point when he wrote that "the interpolation of a shadow" between words and the world "loses all point" once it is appreciated that the "shadows" invite interpretation as much as the words themselves (1960: 37). Kripke, certainly, takes to heart Wittgenstein's advice to "try not to think of understanding [meaning] as a 'mental process' at all" (1969: §154) – though whether he is right to regard Wittgenstein as a meaning-sceptic is a matter of contention.

Wittgenstein's point is at its clearest in connection with the mental *images* that, for some earlier thinkers, serve to fix the meanings of words associated with them. If the term "image" is taken seriously, a real analogy with actual pictures is suggested. But consider how hopeless would be the proposal that the meaning of "An old man is walking up a steep path" is fixed by association with a picture. This is because any picture that might seem to "fit" could just as well represent an old man sliding down the path. "Perhaps a Martian would describe the picture so" (Wittgenstein 1969: 54). The point is not affected if the picture is only a mental one. Whatever the medium – paint, papier mâché, or mind-stuff – the image no less calls for interpretation than the sentence whose meaning it is supposed to decide. Nor is the point affected by considering candidates other than mental images. Consider, for example, the suggestion that what someone means by a word is settled by a mental representation of a rule that he attaches to the word. Whatever the medium of that representation – *sotto voce* speech, "mentalese", brain pattern – it too must be interpreted, applied in one way rather than another. So we would need a further representation to decide the interpretation of the first, and so on and so on.

Here is Derrida's way of conveying the same point. Any mental item proposed for the role of what is signified by a word must "also be in the position of a signifier" itself: like the word, it too represents, applies, can be misapplied, is inferentially connected with other items, and so on. As such, the item is "not simply present" for inspection: the very identity of the item, as the signifier it is, depends on its relations to what is "absent" – to future occasions of its use, for example. But in that case, it is not "transparent", not something that is "nothing other than its presence" – hence not something at which someone can, as it were, take an internal stare so as to settle what the word associated with it means (Derrida 1981: 20, 22, 26).

Those who invoke mental items are, in effect, demanding the impossible from such items. On the one hand, they must, as Wittgenstein puts it (1960: 5), be sufficiently "alive" to "impart life" to what would otherwise be "dead" noises and marks. On the other hand, they must be sufficiently like "mere" – as it were "dead" – objects for inspection of them to determine just what they are. To the extent that they are "alive" – pregnant with future application in as yet undetermined contexts – they invite the same sceptical worries as the word-meanings they were invoked to decide. To the extent that they are "dead", they play no role in explaining how someone uses, and means something by, his words. Either way, it is not by delving inside the head that one discovers the facts, if there are any, that constitute meanings.

Community

Another group of readers will be getting impatient. Let's grant, they will say, that neither "overt behaviour" nor goings-on "in the head" determine meanings. However, there is somewhere else to look – shared, communal practices. A person's understanding what a word or other item means, these readers suggest, is a matter of his employing it in conformity with the community to which he belongs, of his participation in a shared practice. It is this – not the "overt behaviour" of an individual considered in isolation, nor anything occurring "in the head" – that enables determination of a person's meaning and understanding.

The suggestion is initially appealing. After all, in everyday life, a person is typically judged to understand a word when his employment of it conforms to a generally shared practice. When, say, a person uses "+" as the rest of us do, he is normally taken, with no ifs and buts, to understand by it the addition function, and not some bizarre function with which his mathematical feats are also compatible. To be sure, if the suggestion is to persuade, it requires elaboration and qualification. We need to know, for example, what the relevant kind of community is whose shared practice provides the criterion for what individual speakers mean. And, as it stands, the suggestion disallows a possibility that should surely be allowed – that where an individual's application of a word differs from that of the wider community, it may be he, not it, who registers the better understanding of its meaning. Just as Henry Fonda in *Twelve Angry Men* manages to persuade his eleven fellow-jurors that they would be wrong to return a verdict of "Guilty!", so a maverick tribesman might rightly convince his tribe that they are wrong to apply a certain holy word to some object. Maybe they are overlooking an authoritative scripture in which such an application is proscribed.

Unfortunately, the suggestion – even when suitably elaborated and qualified – will fail to disturb the meaning-sceptic. Kripke, for one, happily allows that, often, we may justifiably say of an individual speaker that he understands what a word in our language means. What he denies is that, in saying this, we are truly (or falsely) stating that this speaker means by the word what we – the community – mean by it. This is because, first, we are not, in a full sense, *stating* anything at all, but engaging, legitimately enough, in the socially important "game" of "admitting" someone "as a normal speaker of the language and member of the community". Where the word is "plus", the speaker is "admitted into the community" in his specific capacity "as an adder" (1982: 92). The second, and critical, reason we should not construe "John understands that word" as a statement about John's conforming to what the community means by the word is that there is no such fact as what the community means by it. Think of the community as a single, yet many-tongued, individual. It is then apparent that the sceptic's reasons for denying that an individual speaker means anything determinate by his words apply just as much to this many-tongued super-individual. Assume, in particular, that the sceptic is right to argue that John's linguistic behaviour to date is compatible with his meaning any number of different things by a certain word. It then makes no difference to that argument if, for "John", one substitutes the name of the whole community of which he is a member. For example, "there is but a finite stock of previous uses of '+' by the community, and that no more determines what function was meant than does the individual's past usage" (Hale 1997: 374).

Pertinent to challenging the conviction that there *must* be something determinate that the community means are some reflections of Derrida's. He concedes that, as things stand, there exist fairly "stable" "norms of minimal intelligibility" – ones of the sort, that is, that shape our interpretations, in everyday life, of words and other "signs" employed within a community. It is, he implies, to this stability that the conviction of determinate meanings owes. But that conviction is misplaced: what the stability reflects is not a shared grasp of anything "absolute and ahistorical", such as determinate meanings would be. Rather the relatively stable norms "depend upon socio-historical conditions" and contingent "relations of power" within societies (1988: 147).

Derrida's thought, I take it, is that instability, flux and unpredictable change in how people use and receive words is, as it were, the default position. Where that position obtains – where there is a freer rein for people to apply and respond to words according to their individual perceptions of appropriateness – there would be little pressure to make such assumptions as that usage to date dictates how words must be applied tomorrow, that temporary convergence on a word's application betokens a common understanding, or that when divergence occurs some people are getting things right, the others getting it wrong. In the default position, that is, there would be no pressure on thinking that the community must mean something determinate by their words in order to manage to communicate. Overlaps and rough similarities between people's speech behaviour are enough for tolerably effective communication: one does not have to explain this in terms of determinate conventions and meanings. (See Davidson 1986b for a not dissimilar point. On Derrida, see Spinosa 1992 and Wheeler 1986.) Now the present situation, in organized societies like ours, is not, Derrida is saying, the default one: there is much greater stability, uniformity and predictability in the use of "signs". But this is to be explained in broadly "sociohistorical" terms. Just as, in the wider domain of human actions, our present behaviour is, in part, made more uniform and predictable by the institution of the law, so the present stability of "norms of minimal intelligibility" is due to discernible socioeconomic and cultural factors that put a premium on speaking in concert, in toeing the linguistic line, in speaking – as Heidegger would put it – as "They" speak. The important thing, Derrida warns, is not to be seduced by this current climate of stability into thinking that beneath or behind it – and somehow explaining it – is a battery of determinate meanings that, wonderfully, we all manage to associate with the same words. That climate has not always prevailed and, if Derrida has his way – for "'deconstruction' is . . . destabilization on the move" (1988: 147) – it won't prevail in a future where, once again, the freedom of the default position will be retrieved.

Taming the sceptic?

My account of meaning-scepticism has been sympathetic. Explanations and indications of meaning take many forms, of course, and the sceptic's style of argument does not extend to all of these. His argument applies, primarily, to explanations that indicate what some word or other item means in a person's vocabulary or repertoire of signs. I have agreed with the sceptic that his argument is not threatened by appeals either to what goes on "in the head" or to communal practice. So am I endorsing meaning-scepticism? No: claims to the effect that there is no fact of the matter as to what anyone means strike me as exaggerated statements of a truth that could be more soberly expressed. The sceptic can be tamed, if not put down. That said, there are those, as we'll see, who think that his taming leaves us with an equally dangerous animal.

Let's proceed by exploiting – though for a different purpose – an earlier analogy I drew between meanings and values. (The purpose in Chapter 1 was to highlight the oddity of describing as a theory of meaning the attempt to derive, for each sentence in a language, a statement of its meaning. After all, no one thinks that a theory of, say, moral value is trying to specify, for every action, its moral value.) Several writers have drawn attention to parallels between meaning-scepticism and certain forms of moral scepticism (e.g. Luntley 1991). This is unsurprising given their view that meanings, like values, are "normative" – that, in my terminology, indications both of meanings and of values are judgements of appropriateness. A moral sceptic (or nihilist), it is pointed out, often argues in a manner analogous to that of the meaning-sceptic: consider *all the facts* about a person's action, and you'll see that these are nevertheless compatible with rival evaluations of it – hence no facts can constitute its being the right (or wrong) thing to do. What actually *is* no more determines what someone *ought* to do than his actual speech determines what he means. It may be that, in everyday life, we decide the value of an action by checking its conformity with our communal practice; but that only delays the sceptical verdict, for there are no facts determining the value of that general practice. Compare the pointlessness of invoking the community to refute the meaning-sceptic.

Writers who emphasize such parallels are, typically, critics of meaning-scepticism. What's wrong with it, they argue, can best be appreciated by first exposing parallel flaws in moral scepticism. It just doesn't follow from the point that no amount of "natural" facts entail a particular evaluative judgement that the latter cannot be warranted and even compelling. The judgement will not be true in the sceptic's sense of corresponding to what he allows as facts – but so what? It may certainly be true *qua* fully justified. If the sceptic replies – citing, perhaps, global variations in moral beliefs – that no judgements can be thus justified, he is on dangerous ground. The critic, after all, does not deny that there can sometimes be genuine indeterminacy – that, in some cases, there really can be no strong warrant for deciding among rival moral convictions. What he rejects is the sweeping a priori insistence on a general indeterminacy. By appealing to empirical factors like variation in moral belief, the sceptic is close to conceding that one has to look at particular cases to see whether there is a truth of the moral matter. His critic will add that, in practice, sceptics make their case look stronger than it is by unduly restricting the range of facts germane to moral judgements and their warrant. In particular, scant attention gets paid to our moral *experience* – to, say, our inexpungeable sense, on occasions, of just *seeing* the wrongness in what someone is doing.

In effect, the critic holds, moral sceptics misidentify their target. Their real complaint should be made not against those who claim that there are recognizable moral truths but against a certain conception of moral truth – an "objectivist" or "realist" one according to which a judgement could only be true by corresponding with states of affairs that obtain quite independently of human perspective, sentiment, concern and the like. The sceptic, charges his critic, shares with the objectivist a failure to appreciate that moral truths, if not *sui generis*, are of a different ilk from, say, scientific ones – that perceptions of moral appropriateness are not reducible to some other sort. Once this is appreciated, there is no need to indulge in sceptical or nihilist rhetoric. "There is no fact of the matter as to whether anyone ever acts rightly" turns out to be a grotesque way of recording that, as G. E. Moore might have put it, right actions are what they are and not something else.

A parallel case is levelled against meaning-scepticism. It just doesn't follow from the point that facts about "overt behaviour" and the like do not entail a particular ascription of meaning that the latter is not fully warranted. Kripke, with his construal of "John understands that word" as an endorsement of John's speech – an "admission" of him into our linguistic community – is conceding as much. What is unclear is why Kripke is unwilling to go further. Why not regard whatever warrants the ascription of meaning – the "admission" of the speaker into the community – as justification for saying that it is *true*, even a *fact*, that the speaker means such-and-such? Why, in other words, shouldn't one treat meaning-indications as belonging to one of those domains where, according to a long pragmatist tradition, truth should be understood in terms of warranted assertibility? (In Chapter 3, assertibility-conditions were contrasted with truth-conditions; but that contrast might be redrawn within a broadened notion of truth-conditions – as one between the conditions under which something is justifiably asserted and "transcendent" ones to which some statements may correspond irrespective of our capacity to tell when they do.)

The sceptic may argue that we never in fact do possess the powerful warrant for ascribing meanings that would justify speaking of the truth of such ascriptions. But that is an implausible claim: in everyday life, and by ordinary standards of warrant, we are often and justifiably confident of ascriptions. Of course, if one is as niggardly as Quine with respect to what can count as justifying evidence – rather simple overt linguistic behaviour – the sceptic's claim sounds more plausible. But then we should draw his attention to the rich variety of reasons, operative in everyday life, for ascribing the meanings we do. Like the moral sceptic, the meaning-sceptic typically ignores *experiences*. As Wittgenstein urged, we not only understand meanings but often experience words and other meaningful items *as* meaning what they do (1969: pp. 175ff.). Consider, for example, facial expressions. Typically, I don't form the reasonable belief, inductively based, that her look means she is angry; I am aware of this in her look. Likewise, I don't first hear the noises "Add 2" and then work out that the speaker probably means that I should add 2; rather, it belongs to my experience of the noises that they are a vocalization of that meaning. "We must", writes one philosopher, ". . . learn to characterize experience . . . in such a way that the norms of meaning are already part of the experience" (Luntley 1991: 181). Put differently, it belongs to our experiences of words in use that they are appropriate, or not, for communicating this or that.

The critic's central complaint is that the meaning-sceptic, like his moral counterpart, has misidentified his real target. That target is not the claim that we sometimes truly state what a word or speaker means. It is an objectivist or realist conception of the truth of such statements, according to which it is a truth independent both of our "ongoing use" of words and of the ways, in ordinary practice, that we "ratify" the statements. (The terminology is borrowed from Crispin Wright, e.g. 1980 and 1984.) It is important, here, to guard against a misunderstanding. The point is not that the ways in which we extend words to apply to new cases, and our further reasons for judging that someone knows their meanings, are powerful, even conclusive evidence for *independent* facts as to what the words mean. That would be to resurrect the failed claim that some fact about the mind or about the community constitutes the fact that someone means such-and-such by his words. The point, rather, is that there are no independent facts, that truth, when attributed to statements of meaning, must be *understood* in terms of ongoing use and ratification.

If the critic is right, the sceptic's denial that it is ever true that words and speakers mean anything is a misguided way of expressing the valid point that statements about meanings are, if not *sui generis*, then at any rate not reducible to statements about overt behaviour and the like. The point can be put in terms of appropriateness, thereby recalling the connection with the taming of moral scepticism. To explain, indicate or ascribe meanings is to display or recognize the appropriateness of what is said or done. It should not really be surprising if success or failure in displaying or recognizing appropriateness is something that is not determined independently of practice, perception, perspective and judgement – of the "ongoing use" of words and procedures for ratification included. Looked at this way, the sceptic's mistake is one he shares with the objectivist: that of seeking – and, in the sceptic's case, unsurprisingly failing to find – a way of grounding appropriateness (normativity, if you like) in something entirely different. This is Wittgenstein's point, perhaps, in his frequent insistence that nothing could *tell* us how to speak, that "only the application of language can show how it is to be applied" (quoted in Baker and Hacker 1980: 40). Nothing external, one might say, could confer appreciation of appropriateness on those who lack it. (See Stroud 1996.)

Meaning and world

The preceding section has tamed and reformed the meaning-sceptic into someone who merely denies the objectivity of meanings and their reduction to "natural" facts. "'*Merely*'?! That's a very big 'merely'", will be the response of two (overlapping) groups of philosophers – the friends of objectivism and naturalism respectively. For the latter group, which includes Quine, the resistance of statements about meaning to naturalistic reduction is good enough reason to prefer an untamed meaning-nihilism. After all, isn't the extension of naturalism to all domains, including that of meanings, the biggest "research programme" in town? As for the rejection of objectivism or realism about meanings, doesn't that entail that our speech is "no more than a clacking of hens" or a "brute meaningless sounding off", as Zhuang Zi (1984: Ch. 2) and, 2400 years later, John McDowell (1984: 36) respectively wonder?

With the naturalist's outrage, I have, for reasons given in Chapters 1–2, little sympathy. His reductionist obsession will, of course, look all the odder if the "natural" facts to which he hopes to reduce truths about meaning – if such there be – turn out to be no more objective, no more independent of perspective, than statements about meaning are themselves alleged to be by my tamed sceptic. But while the inflation of anti-realism about meanings into a general anti-realism – parallel to the inflation of meaning-scepticism into global scepticism – would render the naturalistic programme pointless, it is an inflation that makes the objectivist all the more determined to fight his corner. Indeed, it is the prospect of this inflation that causes most consternation – if not to Zhuang Zi, who cheerfully concedes that "there is, in reality, neither truth nor error, ... only ... point of view" (1984: Ch. 2), then certainly to McDowell. He writes that the objectivist "idea of things being thus and so anyway ... requires the conception of how things could correctly be said to be anyway". This, in turn, requires that there be an objective fact of the matter as to how "the pattern of application" of a word "extends" independently of ongoing use and ratificatory procedures (1984: 325). For McDowell, then, global anti-realism – the denial that things are "thus and so anyway" – ensues from anti-realism about meaning. To block the latter, but without embracing a reductionist naturalism, we should think of our understanding of words as akin to a "contractual" agreement.

However great a role interests and practices have played in shaping our vocabulary, once items of that vocabulary are in place, their "patterns of application" – how they will be extended to new cases – are determined in advance and independently of interests and the like. Of course, interests may intervene to alter a pattern; but in such cases, we should conclude that the word's meaning has changed – not that there never was an objective fact of the matter as to what it meant and how, therefore, it *should* have been extended in a manner consonant with that meaning. (On "contractualism", see Hale 1997.)

Before responding to this line of thought, let me record my agreement with the contention that anti-realism about meanings invites a more general anti-realism – one that extends, at the very least, to statements about the "Life-world", the world as we encounter and experience it "in the stream of life". Rightly reminding us of the appropriateness of language to Life, Stephen Mulhall writes that:

> the native speaker's . . . assimilation of the resources of her mother tongue is shown not only in the handiness of its words but in the ways in which the objects of the world as that language articulates them are handy for her, are woven so seamlessly into her practical activity.   (2001: 179)

And he reminds us, too, that this world of "handy" objects is itself one of meaningful, significant items. The allusion, here, is, of course, to Heidegger's point, endorsed in Chapter 2, that the world as "primordially" encountered is the "Life-world" of "handy" (or "ready-to-hand") things that owe their significance and identity to their place in human practices. That world is a "whole of significance" (Heidegger 1980: §32). But in that case, an anti-realist account of meaning must apply to this world as much as to the language used to articulate it. There will not be a way things in the world anyway and independently are if, as meaningful items in a whole of significance, they, as much as words and other signs, owe their meanings – and what they are – to "ongoing use" and "ratification".

Philosophers "outraged" by anti-realism about meanings are right, then, to warn that this position inflates into a wider anti-realism. But should they be outraged at all? One reason for their outrage, hinted at perhaps by McDowell's remarks, strikes me as misplaced. This is the thought that, in the absence of a sense of objectivity and "contractual" obligation, there could only be linguistic anarchy – a free-for-all in which the conditions ensuring sufficient agreement on the use of words for communication to be possible would be eroded. Now it may be, as Derrida fondly anticipates, that in a self-consciously "deconstructivist" era, when confidence in determinacy of meaning has been "exploded", the "norms of minimal intelligibility" required for communication would be less "stable". But Derrida is not envisioning a state of anarchy. And rightly so, for there is no good reason to think that investment in determinacy and objectivity bears prime responsibility for the level of agreement among speakers that communication presupposes. Agreement in the language people use, Wittgenstein remarked, is "not agreement in opinions but in form of life" (1969: §241). Life goes on – even in the "destabilized" era envisioned by Derrida: our sort of Life, that is – and why shouldn't this be enough to guarantee agreement? After all, as Wittgenstein also reminds us (1969: §25), much of our linguistic practice – our "commanding, questioning, recounting, chatting" – is a register, not of fragile, ephemeral conventions, but of a form of life rooted in "our natural history".

Let us, for the final part of this discussion, prescind from the issues of whether anti-realism about meanings inflates into something larger and whether it is a position to cause consternation. Let's focus, simply, on the matter of its plausibility. The case for it is, in my judgement, compelling. Meaning is appropriateness to Life, and it would be extraordinary if the world alone, without the cooperation of Life – of our more-or-less malleable and contingent interests, perspectives, values and projects – settled how and to what our words apply. Extraordinary, that is, if, as contractualists maintain, what shaped our having the concepts and words we do then ceases to play a role in their subsequent careers, in how they are judged appropriately to apply. Jane Heal, who reasonably takes herself to be following Wittgenstein, puts the point well. "To use any concept is to make a move in one sort of life rather than another", so that any use testifies to "the interconnectedness of our concepts, practices and interests". The contractualist idea that the appropriate use of a concept or word "falls entirely on the world" – on how things are supposed anyway to be – is a "will-o'-the-wisp", a product of the misguided conviction that "the real joints at which the world is sliced" is something available to us independently of practices, interests and perspectives (Heal 1989: 226–7, 190, 210).

There is a point that a critic might raise, but which the anti-realist should be happy to concede, for it does not trouble his case. Normally, we do not appeal to Life – to interests, say – in justifying the application of a word. Typically, we say things like "'Dog' applies to that creature because it has four legs, barks and so on", *not* things like "It suits our interests and practices to call that creature a dog". But this only shows that we are, as it were, "passive" when applying words, that we feel compelled by what is before us to label it in one way rather than another. What it cannot show is that our feeling so compelled – and the context of compulsion, as it were – is itself independent of interests and practices. It cannot, for example, show that our impulse to call that creature a dog in virtue of its having such-and-such properties, and despite its dissimilarities in various respects from any other creature hitherto encountered, does not reflect purposes and interests that might have been different and might be different tomorrow.

The point just raised also means that the anti-realist cannot provide clear-cut examples of where interests, rather than the world, dictate how words get applied. Except in cases – familiar in the legal sphere, for example – where it is stipulated, for pragmatic reasons, that a word shall be applied thus and so, we apply them with a sense of having so to apply them. But what can be done is to provide plausible examples of the following: uses of words that might, for reasons plainly related to Life, surely have been different from what, as a matter of fact, they have been and which, had they been different, it would be invidious to denounce as mistaken or as tokening changes in meanings. This, in effect, was Wittgenstein's point about the word "game" (1969: §§66ff.). Had our form of life been somewhat different, the word might have been extended to activities that, as things have turned out, we do not call games. The insistence that the word would then have altered its meaning is a misleading way of registering that, had our interests and perceptions of salience been different, we would have found it appropriate and natural to apply "game" in ways different from those that actually prevail. Again, as I have suggested elsewhere (Cooper 2002: Ch. 5), the ways in which we apply our colour terms – for example, to things even under conditions (e.g. pitch darkness) where they do not *look* to be the colours we describe them as having – reflect practical concerns that might have been less pressing. People for whom such concerns are less pressing would apply colour terms differently, but it would be parochial to regard them as mistaken, as violating some contract. (On colour terms and practical interests, see MacIntyre 1992).

It may be helpful, in conclusion, to retrace the path taken in this chapter. It began by considering the startling sceptical or nihilistic claim that there is no fact of the matter as to what the words in a person's vocabulary mean, for all the gleanable evidence as to what they mean is compatible with any number of hypotheses. I agreed with the sceptic that this argument cannot be overturned by trying to locate the fact of the matter either "in the head" of the speaker or in communal practice. It emerged, however, that the sceptical conclusion was an exaggerated way of denying that the truth of ascriptions of meaning is independent of "ongoing use" and "ratification" – a misleading way, that is, of stating an anti-realist attitude towards meanings. Although that attitude, I argued, cannot be disentangled from a more general anti-realism, it does not, I also argued, carry with it the threat of anarchy that some critics discern.

I then proceeded to defend the anti-realist attitude. It is one that, I suggested, must appeal to anyone already drawn to a conception of meaning in terms of appropriateness to Life. To understand the meanings of words in one's vocabulary is to have a capacity, as Heal put it, to "make move[s] in one sort of life rather than another". It would be surprising if, as the contractualist urged, the proper exercise of that capacity, in applying words, were governed only by how the world is and not, as well, by aspects of the Life in which we engage with the world. It would be surprising, that is, if the interests, ambitions, projects, practices, sensitivities, perceptions of salience, evaluative commitments, sense of what matters and much else that belongs to the fabric of Life served only to shape a vocabulary and not, as well, to constrain and guide its ongoing application. If so, there is no fact of the matter as to what items in this vocabulary mean independently of how participants in that "sort of life" find it appropriate to their Life actually to employ the items. Let me leave the final word to a philosopher whose work has helped prompt my own discussion. Our words, writes Merleau-Ponty, are not a "simple notation" that pictures the given order of things. They are items, rather, "into which the history of a whole language is compressed". But this is a history that cannot be factored out from the larger history of that "fundamental activity whereby man projects himself towards a 'world'" (1962: 188, 191). That ever-unrolling history, the living of Life, is inevitably at work in shaping our judgements of appropriateness and hence our perceptions of meanings.

Meaning, society and
5 the human sciences

In Chapters 3 and 4, the focus has been upon linguistic meaning, salutary though it was at strategic points to recall that meaning is not the monopoly of language. In the remainder of this book, it is no longer the focus. The topic for Chapter 6 is meaning in the arts, plastic and musical no less than literary; while, in Chapter 7, it is the meaning of human life itself that is the subject. In the present chapter, our broad and amorphous domain coincides with the subject matter of the social or human sciences, the *Geisteswissenschaften* – with, *inter alia*, symbolic behaviour, ritual, social role, etiquette and taboo. It is the domain, in effect, that some students of the *Geisteswissenschaften* identify precisely as the context of *meaningful* human behaviour.

It would be wrong, of course, to disjoin this domain from language. Older works, like Darwin's (1873) on the expression of emotions that explain types of human action, such as gestures, as "residues" of merely animal behaviour now look quaint, not least because they ignore the whole new context for behaviour that human language provides. (Are they less quaint, though, than recent "explanations" of human behaviour offered by sociobiologists who, readers may feel, haven't noticed that this is, indelibly, the behaviour of creatures who speak?) It is not simply that words often accompany meaningful actions, or that they are available for describing them; rather, words are typically among the media through which the actions are performed. Appropriate utterances, as much as a prescribed dress or a suitable posture, may be integral to a ceremony or ritual. There are other reasons why reflection on language is not to be set aside. Not only is it characteristic of those social scientists who take the category of the meaningful as fundamental to exploit analogies between linguistic and other behaviour, but the hope is often held out that reflection on specifically linguistic meaning – on criteria of translation, for example – may settle philosophical issues, including that of cultural relativism, that are spawned by the social sciences. Whether or not that hope is misplaced will be the topic for the later sections of this chapter. But it is with the rather different question, indicated by the reference to meaningfulness as a "fundamental" category, that we shall first be concerned.

Battles: phoney and real

One task for an account of meaning, I urged in Chapter 1, is to say something about the "function" of meaning. Or, rather, two tasks, for the question may be about either the role of meaning in human life or the role of the notion of meaning in the study and understanding of that life. The short answer to the first question is that the function of meaning in human life – of producing and understanding meaningful items, of indicating and explaining meanings – is the enabling of human life itself. Ernst Cassirer is right that "we can never penetrate back to the point" when "language, myth, art" and other vehicles of meaning "arose", since they have always been "something already existing" for us (1996: 38). This implies that, without them, we would not be "us" at all – creatures with a distinctively human way of existing.

If meaning is thus fundamental to human life, it might then seem obvious that the notion of meaning enjoys a fundamental role in the human sciences, in the description and explanation of actions and social relations. But it is not obvious, not at any rate to the many social scientists who purport to dispense with the notion. After all, they might argue, the fact that such concepts as grace and miracle play an essential role in a certain religious way of life does not entail that they must figure, except in scare-quotes, in the sociologist's understanding of that way of life. He himself will not, as the participants do, invoke miracles and grace to explain why they act as they do. Why, analogously, should the sociologist or anthropologist deploy the notion of meaning in the explanation and understanding of behaviour just because the actors themselves do so?

We have arrived, then, at an issue which has divided social scientists ever since the fledgling days of their disciplines – whether those disciplines are distinguished from others, notably the natural sciences, through their necessary deployment of the notion of meaning. Unfortunately, the nature of the issue has often been obscure, and certainly it is risky to take at face value all the pronouncements made on it. It is hardly clear, for example, that sociologists who define the meaning of objects and behaviour in terms of the "responses" they cause (see Kerckhoff 1964: 418–19) are concerned with meaning at all, even in the liberal sense urged in this book. For not just any old response to, say, a gesture is germane to its appropriateness or meaning. Conversely, we should not assume that refusals to invoke meaning are what they seem, for the authors may only be rejecting the relevance of some particular conception of meaning. When the author of a book on cultural symbolism declares that symbolic behaviour and beliefs "mean nothing" (Sperber 1975b: 134), his point turns out to be that certain theories of symbolic meaning – semiological, Freudian and so on – are mistaken and that, anyway, in the domain of symbolism, there are not the tight "analytical" relations that, in his view, obtain among those paradigmatically meaningful items, words and sentences. Finally, it is rash to assume that when two social scientists both invoke a notion of meaning it is the same one in each case. When Max Weber argued that explanations of action must be "adequate on the level of meaning", he was urging – against Durkheim, for example – that sociology must heed the "subjective sense" or "subjectively intended meaning" that actions have for the actors (1922: 4–5). For others, adequacy on the level of meaning might instead be a matter of identifying rules or conventions which – perhaps unbeknownst to the actors – their actions instantiate. Or consider the gulf between an anthropologist who holds that "*all* the various non-verbal dimensions of culture, such as styles in clothing, . . . furniture, food . . . and so on are organised . . . so as to incorporate coded information in . . . a manner analogous to . . . a natural language" (Leach 1976: 10) and one who holds that such "dimensions" are unsystematically "evocative" of venerable traditions – symbols of "shared memory", as Borges puts it (1979: 33). Both may speak of the meaning possessed by a bowler hat, a sedan chair or a Christmas pudding, but there agreement ends.

So there are phoney wars and truces in this area. How, then, do we identify the real friends and enemies of meaning in the human sciences and the issues that divide them? One policy is to fix on a narrowly circumscribed characterization of meaning and define the issues as ones about the value or necessity, in these sciences, of the notion thus characterized. This, in effect, was the strategy behind Dan Sperber's claim that symbols "mean nothing". In ordinary speech, he holds, meaning is "confused", albeit "harmlessly", with reference, connotation, diagnosis or whatever. But in "philosophical or scientific exposition", it is crucial to employ a properly "circumscribed" notion. Since this is to be found only in linguistics, the question is whether meaning as defined by certain linguists is usefully or intelligibly deployable by theorists of symbolism and other cultural phenomena (1975b: 8–9).

That policy is not in the spirit of the present book, one of whose messages has been to recognize and respect the wide reach of the notion of meaning. It is quite contrary to that spirit to speak of "confusing" meaning with reference, connotation or diagnosis given that, in suitable contexts, meaning-indications may take precisely the forms of explaining what words and other items refer to, suggest or are symptomatic of (see Chapter 2 above). It is a policy, moreover, with its dangers. One is that the circumscribed notion of meaning is, quite apart from its narrowness, a poor one. (The linguists' notion favoured by Sperber, as it happens, is a dated one that relies heavily on contested concepts like those of analyticity and synonymy.) More seriously, for our purposes, the stipulative policy may occlude the issues on which, historically, champions of meaning in the *Geisteswissenschaften* have been at odds with their rivals. Interesting as some questions about the (dis)similarity between clothes or meals and words may be, it is not this that has been the main bone of contention. What has been is well expressed by Cassirer. Anthropology must, for all its empirical aspects, engage in the "philosophy of meaning". This is because of the bankruptcy of "positivism", whose "leading idea" was that the only proper "explanation" of "all phenomena of human existence and action" is their "subsumption under the general causal structure of becoming" – an idea whose clear implication is that "all questions of sense and meaning" must either be exiled or "brought under this [positivist] point of view" (1996: 36–7).

Cassirer's contention – anticipated by Dilthey, Husserl, Weber and Max Scheler – could be expressed in terms of what is explained by explanations of meaning, namely appropriateness to Life. I take the contention to be that positivist or naturalist attempts to explain the "phenomena of human existence and action" in a way that dispenses with the idea of appropriateness to Life must fail. It is an idea that social scientists cannot abandon, marginalize or subsume under "general causal" notions. When introducing the idea of appropriateness in Chapter 2, I took my lead from Dilthey. It will be useful to recall and elaborate his position, which may serve as a specimen of social theory's friendship with meaning.

Dilthey famously championed the "relative independence" of the *Geisteswissenschaften*, whose "methodology [is] different from that of the physical sciences" (1979: 165, 177). At times, his complaint seems to be that the natural sciences are bound to ignore "the whole man" – both the "real blood flow[ing] in the veins of the [human] subject" and his or her "inner" mental life (*ibid.*: 160ff.). Certainly Dilthey's proposed "methodology" of *Verstehen* (understanding) and empathy has often been interpreted as one of "getting inside" the heads (or veins) of those whose lives the social scientist is trying to explain. But his more considered remarks have a different emphasis. Mental life, including one's own, is intelligible only through the "creations", "objectifications", "projections" and forms of "expression" – artworks, legal systems, religious practices and so on – that manifest human intelligence, will and imagination. It is these objectifications, creations and expressions that are the "subject-matter" of the *Geisteswissenschaften* (*ibid.*: 175–6, 192).

In "a particularly close connection with [the] understanding" sought by these sciences is "the category of meaning", not least because meaning "lies in [the] nature" of the practices and creations examined (*ibid.*: 235–6). Artists, lawmakers, priests understand one another – indeed, themselves – in terms of the meanings of what they make or do. Here, too, Dilthey's considered position belies his occasional tendency to identify these meanings with "mental states" "expressed" by external "signs". Instead, he emphasizes three aspects of enquiry into meanings that render it very different from both the exposure of mental states and the investigations of natural scientists. First, it is akin to understanding written texts – above all because it is dictated by the "holistic" principle that "meaning means nothing except belonging to a whole", so that in the case of meaningful actions, as much as that of texts, "individual parts" must be understood "in terms of the whole" to which they contribute (*ibid.*: 233, 262). Secondly, it is enquiry into an inherently *normative* realm. In grasping the meaning of an action, we grasp how it "commits" a person "for the future" and in terms of purposes whose realization contributes to that of a "supreme good" for the person (*ibid.*: 216, 235).

Finally, the "basis" for the "comparative study" of meaningful action and expression is "Life". "Meaning" is defined in relation to Life, for it "designates the relationship . . . of parts of a life to the whole" of Life (*ibid.*: 232ff.). "Life itself!" is Dilthey's answer to the questions "What is the 'whole' in terms of which meaningful constituents are finally intelligible?" and "What is the 'purpose', ultimately, to which meaningful behaviour is 'committed'?" As the total "context of . . . interactions between people" – as "the human world" – Life is "that behind which it is impossible to go" (*ibid.*: 231f.; 1923–: VII, 359). Life, as the internally connected significant whole in relation to which deeds, events and creations have their meaning, is not to be grasped, like the natural world, in terms of "co-existence or subordination" to causal regularities. The inseparable categories of Life – meaning, purpose, expression, value – "have nothing to do with nature" (*ibid.*: 235, 238).

So there is our specimen of social theory's friendship with meaning. I do not have the space to chart later developments of, and variations on, Dilthey's position. (For a useful overview, see Schwandt 2000.) But it is clear that generations of assorted hermeneuticists, interpretative and phenomenological sociologists, ethnomethodologists, qualitative researchers, "Heideggerians" and "Wittgensteinians" have been united – and for reasons akin to Dilthey's – in insisting on the centrality of meaning to social scientific enquiry and in denying that "the categories of Life", meaning included, may be abandoned or marginalized.

But are they right to deny this?

The idea of a social science

The positivists and naturalists to whom Dilthey was responding argued that the social scientist can and should ascend to the same detached, objective standpoint allegedly occupied by the natural scientist observing, describing and explaining the phenomena of nature. At that Olympian level, no use is made of the categories of Life: to describe phenomena in terms of meaning and value is to do so from a human, "subjective" perspective. People's ascriptions of meanings and values in everyday life are, to speak with Vilfredo Pareto (1935: §7), "experimental facts" or data taken due note of by the social scientist, but transcended at the "logico-experimental" level of scientific description and explanation. At that level, description deploys no concepts foreign to natural science and explanation is in terms of "experimentally" observed empirical regularities belonging, to recall Cassirer's phrase, to "the causal structure of becoming".

Such ambitions prompt the question of whether ascent to the Olympian standpoint is possible in the human or social sciences. (I prescind in this discussion from the question of whether this is possible even in the case of the natural sciences. On that issue see Cooper 2002: Ch. 8). The question is usually treated as a broadly empirical one about the possibility of the social scientist escaping the presuppositions and prejudices with which, as a child of his times and someone "woven" into the fabric of a particular culture, he is burdened. A negative answer to the question, so construed, would indeed show that social scientists are bound to employ the categories of Life. But the demonstration could hardly please the friends of meaning, for the point, in effect, is that these categories are employed *faute de mieux*. The point, indeed, is one familiarly made by natural scientists who look down, in scorn or pity, on the shipwrecked aspiration of sociologists to emulate the physicist or biologist and their consequent need to employ concepts with no place in science "proper".

I shall be concerned, however, with a different construal of the question. My question is whether the *Geisteswissenschaften* can ascend to the Olympian level and still retain their status. The answer of Dilthey and the assorted theorists listed at the end of the previous section is clear: what would be lost through that ascent is the very subject-matter of the *Geisteswissenschaften*. Absent the categories of Life and a social science can no longer "confront us with [what] belongs to it as its theme", as Heidegger would put it (1980: 447). Its "theme" or subject-matter cannot "show up" and be "accessible" from the Olympian standpoint. For, as that latter-day Diltheyan, Peter Winch, puts it, to be seen as "social, as opposed to physical" – say, "*as* social events" – phenomena must be viewed in "their internal connection with a way of living" and as "belonging . . . to a system of ideas or mode of living" (1963: 108f.). The subject-matter of social enquiry is precisely the domain of meaningful actions, events, rituals, relations and so on: hence to proscribe, in the positivist manner, the category of meaning is to expel from social enquiry anything to enquire into.

This doomsday scenario will not, as it stands, impress the positivist and naturalist. Granted, they will reply, our everyday notions of action, social events, rituals and the like are ones of meaningful phenomena – of, in effect, overt, observable happenings *plus* the mental states, ideas or whatever that animate or accompany these happenings. But, they continue in Quinean style (see Chapter 4), just as it was progress in psychology to focus on overt behaviour and ignore what, if anything, goes on in "the mental museum", so it is in the social sciences. Thus reformed, these sciences do not so much lose their subject-matter as deal with suitably regimented and tractable phenomena, apt for properly "logico-experimental" treatment – actions *minus* their "inner" accompaniment, ritual behaviour *minus* its associated "ideas" and so on.

This attempt to salvage, in positivist terms, the subject-matter of the *Geisteswissenschaften* will, in turn, fail to impress the friends of meaning. They will first point out that the attempt rests on a crude and unsatisfactory account of meaning, akin to the "mentalistic" one criticized in Chapter 4. The meaning of a social event, action or ritual is not – except from a special and marginal angle of interest – explained by indicating some "inner" mental accompaniment. More generally, it is wrong to think of meaningful actions as overt behaviour *plus* accompaniments that might be abstracted out and then ignored, leaving us to focus on just the behaviour. Rather, it is their shared meaning that renders different actions ones of the same kind, that makes the behaviour exhibited a significant *type* of behaviour for further inspection and explanation. If one ignores their meaning, then actions, rituals and so on will fail to "show up". As Winch, who speaks of meaning as a function of social rules that govern behaviour, puts it, "criteria of identity" for actions "are necessarily relative to some rule". Social scientific, as opposed to, say, anatomical pronouncements on whether items of behaviour are the same or different "are intelligible only relatively to . . . human behaviour, governed by its own rules" (1963: 83f.). Hence, when a sociologist of positivist persuasion, like Pareto, "explains" baptism in terms of a highly general use of water and other liquids for "purification", he loses sight of what he is trying to explain. A "Christian would strenuously [and rightly] deny that . . . baptism rites . . . were really the same in character" as superficially similar pagan ones. Their "internal connection with a way of living" – their meaning – is quite different (Winch 1963: 108ff.). Moreover, crude though Pareto's classification may be, it too relies – contrary to his positivist programme – on discernment of meaning. Why group *these* uses of water together, while ignoring *those*, except through recognizing that the former have significance as acts of purification?

Winch, I noted, speaks of meaning in terms of rules. But, like Wittgenstein, whom he follows, he uses the notion of a rule in a very broad manner – so there is no good reason to interpret him as wedded to the kind of rule-governance account of meaning I criticized in Chapter 3. Indeed, his talk of meaningful behaviour's "internal connection with a way of living", and of actions being meaningful or "symbolic" in virtue of the normative "commitments" and purposes they register, suggests that he would be happy to characterize meaning in terms of appropriateness to Life, to "the context of . . . a given form of social life" (MacIntyre 1973: 18).

One might pull the above considerations together in glancing at a typical case of behaviour that calls for social scientific understanding and explanation. In her memoirs, *Out of Africa*, Karen Blixen speculates on the seemingly puzzling behaviour and attitude of the Kikuyu towards white expatriates like herself:

> I myself think that [they] were afraid of us more in the manner in which you are afraid of a sudden terrific noise . . . And yet it was difficult to tell, for [they] were great at the art of mimicry . . . in the end their behaviour to us might be some sort of strange joke, and the shy people were not afraid of us at all.
>
> (Blixen 1982: 26)

Winch would surely be correct to denounce as hopeless the attempt to explain what is going on by subsuming it under "empirical generalizations" established from an Olympian standpoint where no appeal to meaning and other categories of Life are allowed to intrude. To begin with, Blixen – in order even to have posed her question – must have recognized what was, *prima facie*, shy behaviour, and that is already to have made a judgement about significance. For it can hardly be pretended, given the cultural variations in its forms, that acting shyly is something that would hit the detached physiologist or anatomist in the face. Second, her speculations require deployment of concepts like "joking" and "mimicry" that, once again, collect items of behaviour in virtue, not of any overt similarities, but of shared commitments, purposes and senses of appropriateness. Finally, Blixen's two possible explanations of the Kikuyu behaviour each invoke its relation to, and appropriateness to, the wider whole of their form of life. The first – that the behaviour is akin to fear of natural phenomena, like terrific noises – invites reflection on the behaviour's connection to their vision of white people as similar, in some respect, to natural forces. The second – the "joke" hypothesis – invites us to reflect on the behaviour's connection to a whole "artistic" practice central to tribal life. What such reflections, replete with the categories of Life, might deliver, I don't know; but without them, one has no idea what explanations in some other possible style purport to explain.

"The universality of hermeneutics"

The reference to explanations in a different style may seem to open up a line of attack on the friends of meaning. While the positivists were wrong to dispense entirely with the categories of Life, they correctly envisaged a level of causal explanation to which social scientists should, in much of their work, aspire. What Dilthey, Winch and others regard as "the whole task of the social sciences", complains Alasdair MacIntyre, is only their necessary "starting-point" (1973: 26). We must indeed invoke meanings even to identify what calls for explanation, but once identified this may call for explanation in a different key. This is the case wherever there is a palpable gap between what people do and their own understanding of what they are doing and why. Especially problematic for those, like Gadamer, who defend the "universality" of hermeneutic understanding – its explanatory deployment "all the way down" – are cases where not only is there this gap, but the self-understanding of the actors is "systematically distorted", as when they are in the grip of ideology or "false consciousness". Here, charges Jürgen Habermas, hermeneutic explanation must prove "inadequate", for the distorted understanding itself calls for explanation and in terms, necessarily, other than itself. The social theorist must then turn to "systematic explanation", appealing, for example, to underlying economic conditions that, without any awareness on the actors' part, shape their thinking and behaviour (Habermas 1980: 191).

It is important, in assessing this criticism, to distinguish substantial from verbal issues. The critics need not demand that, at the level of "systematic explanation", the sociologist eschew the vocabulary of meaning. He may, for example, speak of a "distorted" ideology as "expressing" – since it is symptomatic of – economic conditions, or talk of certain behaviour as "significant" because it contributes, unknown to the actors, to satisfying some "unacknowledged needs" of theirs. The critics' point, however, is that this vocabulary is not what it was in the mouths of the true friends of meaning. Expression, significance and so on are no longer tied, as they were for the friends, to the self-understanding of the actors, their capacity to explain meanings, and their sense of acting appropriately or not. In effect, the critic places the friends in a fork. Given the "gaps" and "distortions" referred to above, they must either concede that the categories of Life should be left behind at a certain and unavoidable level of explanation, or concede that, if retained, they must be redefined so as no longer to be foreign to those of causal, systematic explanation.

If, for example, it turns out that putatively "symbolic" behaviour is explicable only in terms entirely foreign to the participants, then the choice is between abandoning the terminology of symbolism and severing any link between symbolic behaviour and the participants' own understanding of what they are up to. Again, if it emerges that kinship regulations among a nomadic people are only explicable as unplanned adaptations to economic necessities, then either the hope must be abandoned that the regulations can be understood in terms of appropriateness to Life, or the connection between appropriateness and normativity must be broken, with appropriateness now "naturalized" and defined in terms of adaptive function.

The critics' substantial charge, then, is that the friends of meaning have grossly exaggerated the constraints that participant or native understanding places upon social scientific understanding and explanation. In many areas of enquiry, we should not remain within those constraints, but "move to another level". Whether or not we retain the husk of a hermeneutic vocabulary, we should be asking not what something "means for the agents themselves", but "what necessary needs and purposes it serves" (MacIntyre 1973: 32).

The critics are right to allege that Diltheyan *Geisteswissenchaft*, with its insistence on the universality of hermeneutic enquiry, is constrained, "all the way down", by agent understanding. But the friend of meaning will accuse his critics of misconstruing this constraint – of, in effect, foisting on him a "mentalism" that equates meaning with what is explicitly "in the heads" of the agents. Gadamer, for one, stresses that the understanding which hermeneutical reflection "brings before me" may be something that "otherwise happens *behind my back*" (1977: 38). What is brought before me can come as *news*. Winch, similarly, denies that the "commitments" in virtue of which an action has sense must be transparent to the actor. Their claim is this: actions and other social phenomena have meaning when what count, in the society, as explanations of meaning do or could identify their meaning. This formulation allows for looser, more complex, but less constrictive relations between meaning and consciousness than the one foisted on the friends of meaning by their critics.

Once this is seen, one appreciates the force of Gadamer's rhetorical question, "Who says that . . . so-called real factors are outside the realm of hermeneutics?" (*ibid.*: 31) – where by "real factors" he has in mind those "unacknowledged needs" and the like, allegedly beyond the ken of agents, to which the critics refer when offering Olympian, causal explanations of social phenomena. Only when, Gadamer is implying, the realm of hermeneutics is equated with what is registered "in the heads" of agents does it seem obvious that these "real factors" are beyond the scope of hermeneutics and the categories of Life. With that equation rejected, it becomes possible either to accommodate a "systematic explanation" within the realm of hermeneutics or to deny, with reason, that it provides explanation at all.

Two related thoughts support this contention. First, if, as MacIntyre suggests, the "real factors" explanatory of certain practices are "needs and purposes" functionally served by the practices, then they are not factors that the participants are themselves incapable of acknowledging. Nor is the appropriateness of these practices something the participants are unable to appreciate. (Acknowledgement and appreciation may not, of course, be under the descriptions – economic jargon, say – used by the social scientist.) For needs and purposes – *human* ones, at least – do not exist independently of their recognition as such. The idea that there are needs of which the needy are hopelessly ignorant is unattractive. It is implausible, for example, to insist that ascetics *must*, despite their disavowals, have sexual needs. It is true that people may disguise their needs and purposes from themselves. But, as that way of putting it suggests, we are then dealing with motivated self-deception or "bad faith": something that, as Sartre saw (1957: Ch. 2), is intelligible only in terms of people's meaningful "projects". For bad faith to be at work, there must be enough in a person's behaviour to show that he or she at some level acknowledges what they then attempt to blot out.

Secondly, it needs to be emphasized more than it sometimes is by "functionalists" that the "real factors" are supposed to explain *human* practice, not the kind of adaptive behaviour also discernible in plants or fish. It is practice for which the agents offer their own explanations, even when these amount to little more than appeals to tradition and ancestral ways. (Parenthetically, though, are participants as ignorant as they are often portrayed by social scientists of the functional advantages of their practices? Do nomads really fail to recognize the advantages of polygamy for communities like their own?) Now, either their own explanations can accommodate the "real factors" or they cannot. If they can – if they share a sense of those factors and their significance – then this is why the factors properly figure in explanation of practice. If they cannot – if these factors cannot be "taken up" into participant understanding of their form of life – then why suppose that anything is explained by exposing those factors? Why not instead say, simply, that the social scientist has observed the "co-existence" or correlation of a "real factor" with a certain social practice? That correlation is no explanation, rather an invitation to explanation in terms of how that factor is taken up into the Life of the agents.

An example might help. Many writers, including T. E. Lawrence, have noted the co-existence of monotheistic religion with harsh, arid landscape and climate. But it would be hopelessly crude to say that people adopt monotheism because they live in such habitats, and to leave it at that. Clearly a *story* needs to be told that renders intelligible, in terms of people's own sense of their environment and its significance, their embrace of the one God. Lawrence's own speculation invokes desert peoples' sense of "the emptiness of the[ir] world", compensated for by a sense of "the fullness of God", and their perception of "the weakness of earth's life mirrored [in] the strength of heaven" (1969: 39, 524). It doesn't matter, for our purposes, if those particular speculations are on target, but at least they are of the right kind. In Gadamer's terms, Lawrence's desert peoples bring "real factors" – of climate and environment – into the realm of hermeneutics. It is not the factors *per se*, but the incorporation into Life of a sense of their significance and of what they call for by way of appropriate response that figures in anything deserving of the name "explanation". That is why, as the friends of meaning insist, hermeneutic understanding must go "all the way down".

"The very idea of a conceptual scheme"
The preceding sections have addressed the role of meaning in the *Geisteswissenschaften* at large. The remaining ones concern how considerations of meaning might contribute to resolution of a philosophical issue prompted by, more particularly, social anthropology.

A main inspiration during the eighteenth century for the pioneers of anthropology was travellers' tales of exotic societies whose beliefs, manners and morals were radically different from those countenanced by Enlightenment thought. Some Enlightenment figures, like Hume, gave short shrift to such tales: "so readily and universally do we acknowledge a uniformity in human motives and actions" that we may dismiss the tales "with the same certainty" as "stories of centaurs and dragons" (1977: 55–6). Hume may well have perceived the spectre of a relativism that would threaten if the tales were credited. If other human beings manage successfully to cope with their world by belief-systems alien to our own, what besides invidious chauvinism could persuade us that we, rather than they, have got the world aright? Hume has had many followers in the attempt to cut the ground from beneath the feet of cultural relativism by denying that the radical conceptual differences alleged by travellers or anthropologists are genuine. South American natives, asserts Claude Lévi-Strauss, cannot think so differently from us, since "the human mind, unconcerned with the identity of its occasional bearers, manifests in that operation a [universal] structure" (1966: 58).

It is not with appeals to a universal human nature, however, that I shall be concerned. Pioneering philosophical anthropologists, like Herder and the brothers Humboldt, recognized that, if there are rival conceptual schemes across the globe, then these will be embodied in peoples' different languages. Hence the possibility of rival schemes requires the possibility of radically different languages. And here, it has seemed to some, is an opportunity to scotch the hypothesis of alternative schemes. In his paper "The very idea of a conceptual scheme", Donald Davidson writes that "two people[s] have different conceptual schemes if they speak languages that fail of intertranslatability." No such failure, he adds, can be envisaged, however, since whatever evidence suggests that the noise-making of some people was not translatable into our language would also be "evidence that that . . . activity was not speech behaviour" (1984: 185). If the natives employ a language or conceptual scheme at all, it must be pretty much like ours; other-wise we couldn't translate it and the assumption that we were confronted by a genuine language should be dropped. If, in a particular case, that assumption is well founded, then the anthro-pologist who attributes to his interlocutors too many weird and wonderful beliefs beyond our ken must eventually concede that he is mistranslating their speech.

There, then, is a quick argument, based on an appeal to meaning and translation, for denying the very possibility that relativists exploit. Too quick, many will say. At the very least, one wants to know what conception of translation is at work here: on some conceptions, it is either palpably wrong to suppose that, where translation fails, there is no intelligible language or conceptual scheme, or trivially correct to suppose this. Consider the two alternative notions of translation offered by the anthropologist Godfrey Lienhardt – the provision of "simple equivalents" for the native words and "making the coherence [their] thought has . . . clear in our own [language]" (quoted in Hahn 1973: 209). Failure

of translation in the second sense does not explain the unintel-
ligibility of the natives, but simply redescribes it. As for the first
sense, neither success nor failure in providing "simple equivalents"
settles the issue of intelligibility. The native language may be inter-
pretable, but of such an unusual syntactic character as to preclude
the equivalence of its terms with ones of ours. Conversely, the assertions attributed to the natives on the basis of "simple equivalents"
may be so bizarre that, as they stand, we can't make sense of them
– for example (Malinowski's), the Melanesian assertion "We run
front-wood ourselves . . . we see behind their sea-arm" (quoted in
Rescher 1980: 327).

Davidson, to be sure, does invoke a conception of translation
which, he believes, obviates these difficulties. Translation begins,
and fundamentally remains, a matter of pairing whole native
assertions with ones of our own – a practice that allows, where necessary, for using English words that have no "simple equivalents" in
the native one. But what warrants a scheme of pairings? What
shows that our assertions bear the meaning of theirs? Nothing more
nor less, according to Davidson, than overall convergence in *truth-
value*. The "guiding policy" of the translator must be to assign, "as
far as possible", to their "sentences . . . conditions of truth that
actually obtain (in our opinion) just when the[y] hold those sentences true" (1984: 196). Where, consequently, there is no good
explanation of native "error", we must reject any translation
scheme that renders the natives as holding true too many sentences
that we reject, or as holding false too many that we accept. It
follows that any language we can translate – and there are no others
– must be that of a people whose beliefs broadly coincide with our
own. Since an alternative conceptual scheme would consist of
beliefs that did not so coincide, there can be no such scheme. A
truth-conditional account of meaning and translation guarantees
that there is "no intelligible basis on which it can be said that
schemes are different" (Davidson 1984: 198).

This counter-intuitive conclusion has, unsurprisingly, been
resisted. It is sometimes pointed out, for example, that we may have
very good evidence, of a behavioural sort, for crediting people with
the use of a genuine language and a system of beliefs even when we
have no idea how to translate their utterances. But that point, as it
stands, will not disturb Davidson, who will reply that the evidence,

if sound, can only be evidence for the possibility – as yet unactualized – of hitting upon suitable pairings of their assertions with ours. A more telling objection is that Davidson misconstrues the kind of putative difference between Them and Us which provokes talk of alternative conceptual schemes. Nicholas Rescher's statement of this objection is hard to better:

> The most characteristic and significant sort of difference between one conceptual scheme and another . . . does *not* lie in the sphere of *disagreements* or *conflicts* . . . arising when the one . . . holds something to be *true* that the other holds to be *false*. Rather, it arises when the one scheme is committed to something that the other does not envisage at all – . . . that lies outside [its] conceptual horizons.   (Rescher 1980: 333)

That sounds right. When, for example, the Dorze of Ethiopa go about "feeding their ancestors", they do something that is not within our horizon of thought, rather than something – like an English child's trying to feed its doll – that betrays ignorance of certain empirical facts.

In what follows, I do not exactly ignore this important point: in a way it informs my discussion. But I want to shift the critical emphasis on to cases where, if Davidson is right, reference to alternative conceptual schemes is *clearly* impermissible, precisely because translation of the Davidsonian ilk has been secured. The general point that will emerge is that Davidson's truth-conditional criteria for sameness of meaning are overly narrow. That sameness of meaning by his criteria obtains does not exclude difference of meaning – of conceptual scheme – by other respectable criteria. (The point will not surprise anyone sympathetic to my claim, in Chapter 3, that specification of truth-conditions is but one, not especially privileged, mode of meaning-indication.)

Translation and difference

One might begin by remarking that, in plenty of cases where talk of different conceptual schemes is invited, adequacy of translation is not at issue. No one, Ian Hacking (1982) has observed, supposes that the Italian or German spoken by Renaissance alchemists and magi presents a major problem of translation; but that hardly scotches the temptation to speak of their bizarre pronouncements as belonging to a scheme of thought that is beyond our contemporary horizons. There are, I suggest, at least three reasons why success in Davidsonian translation – in pairing Their truths with ours, Their falsehoods with ours – fails to exclude that Their scheme of thought is radically unlike ours. Unlikeness may show up in ways other than disagreement over the truth-values of assertions.

The first reason is indicated by Hacking when reflecting on alchemy. The challenge, he writes, is not "to learn systems of translation but chains of reasoning . . . Even after Paracelsus is translated into modern German, one still has to learn how he reasoned in order to understand him" (1982: 60) – to grasp, say, how he could conclude that mercury is a cure for syphilis from the assumption that the planet Mercury "signs" the marketplaces in which, supposedly, the disease was contracted. Doubtless, Paracelsus held true plenty of propositions that we now hold false; but that isn't the issue that tempts one to speak of his operating with a different conceptual scheme. Rather, it is one of strikingly different senses of relevance and appropriateness. How could it have seemed natural to move from considerations about planets to medical remedies? It is no use replying "Because he believed some very odd propositions", since such beliefs could only appear attractive in the very context of thought – and against the very background of relevance – that we are trying to understand.

A second reason is prompted by another of Karen Blixen's observations on the Kikuyu:

> The Europeans . . . complain . . . that the Natives know nothing of gratitude, and that it is the same whatever you do to them . . . It is an alarming quality: it seems to annul your existence as an individual . . . as if you were a phenomenon in nature . . . [like] the weather. (Blixen 1982: 115)

If the Europeans' complaint is right, then the Africans indeed conceive of people – the Europeans themselves, at least – in a manner alien to us. In a good sense, they cannot mean what we mean by "person". But the relevant point is that this difference is one that would remain unexposed by Davidsonian translation. For it is not, presumably, that the Kikuyu *assert* things like "You Danes and English are not people, but natural phenomena", and refuse to assert things like "That was kind of you". Indeed, we might assume that there is nothing that we would assert and they wouldn't, and nothing that we wouldn't and they would. Rather, the profound differences between them and us show up in the way they say things (with detachment, for example), in demeanour and facial expression, in their surrounding behaviour – and so on. The differences intimate, as Wittgenstein would put it, different "scenes" for the language-games – of gratitude, resentment and the like – that they and we respectively play: scenes sufficiently at variance for us to question whether their practices and words have the meaning of ours.

The final reason has to do with the metaphorical and symbolic. Suppose it has been established, given our knowledge of the native language *plus* the "charitable" principle that its speakers rarely hold true what is blatantly false, that some of the utterances to which they subscribe must be construed metaphorically. It is no objection to our translational scheme that the sentences uttered come out, in English, as patent falsehoods, since very generally the sentences used by speakers of metaphor *are* glaringly false. What this entails is that Davidsonian criteria of translational adequacy will fail to exclude radical conceptual difference when, so to speak, the vehicle for a different way of conceptualizing is metaphorical or symbolic speech. Now, especially in the case of concepts that are hard directly to spell out – God, goodness, happiness, the mind – it is precisely through examining webs of relatively systematic metaphors in which they are enmeshed that we appreciate how they are understood. It is clear, moreover, that these – the "metaphors we live by", as the title of a book devoted to the subject calls them (Lakoff and Johnson 1980) – differ significantly across cultures. One thinks, for example, of how a distinctively Western conception of happiness is borne by metaphors of "feeling on a high", "being up", "getting a buzz", "being on top of the world", "bursting out" and so on – ones entirely missing, I am assured, from the rhetoric of certain other, somewhat more Lotus-eating, cultures.

There is, parenthetically, some irony in invoking the figurative in support of the thesis of alternative conceptual schemes, since this is something more usually associated with anthropologists who are trying to protect their interlocuters from attributions of alien concepts. Such attributions, they argue, result from a failure to recognize that the natives are speaking only figuratively. ("When they say 'We are feeding our ancestors', what they *really* mean is that they are honouring the ancestors with symbolic gifts" – that sort of thing.) Doubtless, this strategy is often appropriate, but it will do nothing to dispel the impression that alien concepts are at work if the ways of metaphorizing are themselves alien to our own.

If I am right, then success in Davidsonian pairings of native with domestic assertions is insufficient to guarantee community of conceptual schemes. For radical difference may show up, not in what the natives assert and deny, but in the "scene" and manner of their speech, in their chains of reasoning and sense of relevance, and in their repertoires of metaphor and symbolism. There are two different ways, in connection with the notion of meaning, in which that conclusion might be expressed. One way – that of those wedded to a truth-conditional notion – is to say that similarities of meaning between native utterances and our own may mask great differences in thought and conceptual scheme. The other – that of people not so wedded – is to say that great differences of meaning (and hence of thought and conceptual scheme) may be masked by similarities of the conditions under which They and We hold sentences to be true or false. The second way will be more congenial to those who agree with me that specification of truth-conditions is just one mode of indicating meanings. They will, for example, find it entirely natural to say that those who metaphorize happiness very differently from ourselves mean, for that very reason, something different by happiness. Or that Blixen's Kikuyu mean something different from us by "Thanks!" In both cases, one might say, we are confronted with a Life different from our own: one that provides a different context for the natives' words, a different sense of what their words are appropriate to.

I close with two remarks, the first in response to the question whether the differences whose possibility I have defended amount to the radical differences in conceptual scheme that, from Hume to Lévi-Strauss and Davidson, so many authors have wanted to deny. Well, they are surely significant differences, and of just the sort to which many anthropologists and historians of ideas have drawn attention under the label of "alternative conceptual schemes". The label itself, of course, is not especially important; but it is important to have tried to show that differences of the sort that have intrigued actual anthropologists, rather than writers of science-fiction or fairy-tales, may be for real. If it is only against the speculations of the latter that an argument like Davidson's is effective, then it is of less moment to philosophy and social science alike than its champions imagine.

My second remark is in response to someone who assumes that, in defending the possibility of alternative conceptual schemes, I must also be defending cultural relativism. There is no "must" here. Relativism would be an uninteresting speculation unless there were different schemes to which truth, validity or whatever might be relative; but one does not establish a doctrine by showing that something which it presupposes indeed obtains. It would be beyond the scope of this book to consider the pros and cons of relativism, since these – many of them, at least – lie outside the scope of an examination of meaning. So I abdicate from discussing relativism further, but with just this one parting thought. I accused Davidson of deploying a conception of meaning too narrow to exclude the possibility of radically different conceptual schemes. Arguably, a similar accusation of narrowness may be levelled against some defenders of cultural relativism.

In a notorious passage of *The Idea of a Social Science*, Winch writes that "one cannot apply criteria of logic to modes of social life as such", for each mode – religion, say, or science – "has criteria of intelligibility peculiar to itself" (1963: 100). (I recall, in this connection, a talk in which Winch asserted that there can be no rational criteria, transcending particular "modes of social life", by which to condemn *suttee*.) I suspect that the explanation of this passage is Winch's taking rather literally his talk of meaning as what is determined by the rules of language-games. Certainly, that explains, to jump across the Channel, Jean-François Lyotard's (1986: 52) contention that no discourse may be "legitimated" at the expense of another, since each discourse is a "game" whose rules of intelligibility are "specific to each particular kind". If, for example, the notion of evidence is determined by whichever "game" it is employed in, then it will make no more sense for a scientist to complain about the priest's criteria of evidence than for a soccer referee to object to a rugby referee's criteria of a foul.

I argued, in Chapter 4, that, while meaning-indications some-times take the form of specifying a rule governing the use of a term, it is wrong to suppose that, in general, application of words is deter-mined by rules. This makes the image of language-games, when taken to suggest that discourses are hermetically sealed off from one another, like different sports, by the internal rules that govern them, an unappealing one. To the extent, therefore, that relativism of the ilk defended by Winch and Lyotard relies on that image, it is something for which a more rounded account of meaning affords no support.

6 Meaning and the Arts

"But what does it mean?" Who has not heard, or indeed raised, that question on such occasions as standing before an unmade bed in an art gallery, or listening to a piece called "Invention VI for Oboe and Synthesizer"? The vocabulary of meaning is pervasive in contemporary discussion of art, and not only of the literary arts that inherit familiar issues of linguistic meaning and generate several more of their own, like that of authorial authority over the meaning of a text. Few books on the philosophy of music, for example, are without their chapter on meaning in music.

There's no doubt that the broad issue which has dominated is that of the kind(s) of meaning possessed by artworks, and the bulk of this chapter will be duly devoted to that. But it is not the only one. Possession is not the sole relation that an artwork can bear to meaning. Questions may be asked as well about meanings as, so to speak, the subject-matter of art – as what art may reveal or communicate *about*. This will be the topic for the first section. The two topics are not unrelated, for those who think that art is uniquely equipped to reveal dimensions of meaning are apt to see, in that revelation, an important dimension of art's own significance. The meaning of certain artworks may show up, as it were, through their showing up the meanings of whatever they are "about". The significance that Proust's great novel has for many of its readers surely owes to its author's extraordinarily keen anatomy of a world of meanings – those of gestures, flower-arrangements, the ribbons in a girl's hair, a slice of cake, or whatever: a world that, though a literary creation, is one from whose exploration we easily return, our sensitivity to meanings enhanced, to our own world.

On philosophy's leisurely time-scale, concerns of both the types just mentioned are "modern". They seem not to have taxed the eighteenth-century pioneers of aesthetics, such as Francis Hutcheson and David Hume. It would be too crude, perhaps, to ascribe to those pioneers the twin views that art is there only to please and that it does so, essentially, by "representing" things. But they rarely question a broadly hedonistic conception of art or enquire into modes of meaning beyond representation. Changes in the cultures of both philosophy and the arts were required for concerns about meaning-and-art to become prominent. One thinks, in connection with the first, of the powers assigned to art – well beyond that of pleasing us – by Hegel and his Romantic con-temporaries. In connection with the latter, one thinks of the grow-ing elevation around the same time – and hardly coincidentally – of "pure" music over music that was neither "programmatic" nor an accompaniment to the word: music which was not representational and, in the case of, say, Beethoven, poorly appreciated by those who heard it only – or at all – as "pleasurable". Later developments, ranging from the rise of phenomenology to the "crisis" in represen-tational painting occasioned by the camera (still and moving), will get their mention in due course. But I shall be less attentive to the reasons for the contemporary entrenchment of issues of meaning-and-art than with the fact of that entrenchment.

Art as disclosure

Greatest among the powers assigned to art by Romantic theorists was a transcendental, metaphysical one. Art more than reason, remarked Schelling (1978: 232), "brings . . . man to . . . knowledge of the Highest". The great artist does nothing so humdrum, certainly, as representing this or that object; rather, his works communicate "essence". "I do not paint women", claimed Degas, "I paint Woman!" But there are different versions of the broad idea that art is philosophy conducted by other means, and of particular interest to us is the affiliation of art with phenomenology – for it is integral to this philosophical tendency to articulate and render salient that realm of meaning which Husserl and his followers called "the life-world". Art that is continuous with phenomenology, therefore, will be in the business of disclosing meanings.

This is precisely the claim made by Merleau-Ponty. True visual art, like "true philosophy" – phenomenology, that is – "consists in relearning to look at the world" in all its meaningfulness. That is why art, like philosophy, is "the act of bringing truth into being" (1962: xx). Ironically, a great artist like Cézanne may bring home to us the impregnation of our everyday world with meanings by depicting things in abstraction from "the context of our everyday concerns" and "ordinary preoccupations". Precisely by depicting something as "hostile and alien . . . a resolutely silent Other", Cézanne induces a contrasting sense of how, in ordinary "preoccu-pied" experience, our traffic is with things in their meaning for us (*ibid.*: 322). This is not the only way a Cézanne can induce a sense of meaning. Through "the very organization of its sensible aspects" – colour, tactile value, shape and so on – the canvas may demon-strate how these aspects are "mutually significatory", inseparable from one another. We recognize, for example, that *this* particular colour is identifiable only as that of a certain woollen carpet: not a bare sense-datum, but an aspect "pointing to" or "signifying" an array of other aspects that constitute the "unity" or "fullness" of an object (1962: 323).

Again the artist may, by presenting something in an original way, "summon one away" from the "sedimented" or "already consti-tuted reason" within which we are usually "content to shut" our-selves (Merleau-Ponty 1964: 19). By fracturing our ordinary, clichéd understanding of things, a fresh range of their significance is opened up. (Compare Mark Rothko: "The familiar identity of things has to be pulverized in order to destroy the . . . associations with which our society . . . enshrouds" them (Harrison & Wood 1992: 564).) In Ravel's *La Valse*, for example, the eponymous dance is no longer a romantic pastime, but the expression of a whole culture – a European world – whose destruction during 1914–18 is registered in the disintegration of that dance form. In Van Gogh's famous painting, the shoes are not just boots that are made for walking but, as Heidegger puts it, the "disclosure" of the whole "world and earth" – "the dampness and richness of the soil", "the loneliness of the field-path", "the impending childbed", "the surrounding menace of death" – of "the peasant woman" whose shoes they are (1993: 160). As we saw in Chapter 2, for Heidegger things are significant through "referring" us to other things and, ultimately, to the whole context, the "relational totality", of Life in which they have their place. But it is not by looking at a pair of actual shoes – things taken for granted and "inconspicuous" as we put them on and take them off – that a sense of this appropriateness to Life is aroused. "It is only in the picture that we notice all this about the shoes" (1993: 160). It is precisely by looking at the shoes as depicted by Van Gogh – outside the ordinary context of our everyday concerns and preoccupations – that we "relearn" to experience the total context of meaning to which the shoes owe their significance and identity.

So far, the phenomenologists' point about the meaning-disclosive power of art lends itself nicely to articulation in terms of appropriateness. Meaning is what explanations of meaning indicate, and that is appropriateness to Life; but indication of meaning does not have to take the form of discursive explanation. Suitable gestures and pointings may also indicate – and so may artworks through displaying or showing up relations of appropriateness. Waltz themes of the kind quoted, as it were, in Ravel's *La Valse* before he disintegrates them, are appropriate to – and signify – a certain type of culture in a way that other dances would not have been. Shoes of the type depicted by Van Gogh, similarly, are peculiarly appropriate to the "world and earth" of the peasant. Talk of appropriateness, here, is required to capture the normative character of the relations. The waltz and the shoes are "just right" for referring us to their respective worlds or forms of life that, to speak with Heidegger, they "gather" around them: others would be "all wrong". It's not simply that they are "associated" with those worlds, or have some function in them. For all I know, some sort of maypole-dancing was more popular than the waltz in the Austro-Hungarian empire; but it could not signify the imperial world in the way the waltz does. Again, one might imagine that, due to a leather shortage, peasants were forced to wear surplus army boots or ballet pumps; but these could not evoke the world of the peasant in the way Van Gogh's shoes do. (Art historians tell us that, actually, the shoes in the Van Gogh painting were not a peasant's, but probably the painter's own walking boots. No matter: they remain "just right" for referring us to the peasant's world.) So a musical composition or a painting may indicate meaning, for it may display the meaningful relations of appropriateness in which the things they present stand to Life.

This claim is not contradicted, once allowance is made for exaggeration, by Heidegger's claim that "great art" does not so much *disclose* relations of appropriateness to a form of life as create or "set up" that form. It is, he writes, works like the Greek temples and tragedies that "first give . . . to things their look" and identity for the Greeks, and give to them "their outlook on themselves", their unity and very existence as "a historical people" (1993: 167–8). How can such a work, therefore, *disclose* relationships of appropriateness when it has itself produced them? But Heidegger indeed exaggerates. He cannot really think that the Greeks' form of life sprang into being only through the perceptions afforded by the artworks, for no such works could have been produced by a people not already constituted by a shared and sophisticated culture. Toned down, Heidegger's is the important point that "great art" expands, modifies and deepens a people's "outlook on themselves", and in that respect transforms their Life (see Young 2001). But this is compatible with thinking of such artworks as indicating appropriateness. We should not think of the Life to which practices, including art, are appropriate as something fixed independently of those practices. A genre of religious painting, say, may be palpably suited to the consciousness of an age while, at the same time, modifying and honing that consciousness. To recall the Heideggerian wordplay mentioned in Chapter 2, what is appropriate *to* may also serve to appropriate. "Art", he writes, "belongs to the [*ap*]*propriative event* [*Ereignis*]" (1993: 210) – to that which gives to something an essential nature of its own (*eigen, propre*). Artworks that are suited to a culture may come, as it were, to suit that culture more exactly to what they themselves express.

Nor, I think, is serious qualification to the phenomenologists' claim about art-and-meaning forced by the familiar perception that the aim of much art in modern times is to communicate *loss* of meaning in our world – the atrophy, as one author puts it, of "a comprehensive framework of meaning in which the individual has his allocated place" (Kermani 2002: 15). There is no paradox, once we distinguish between different modes or focuses of meaning, in referring to the significance of the pointless actions and speech of characters in a Beckett play – to the meaning of the meaningless. One way, after all, to explain the significance of what people are doing is to indicate the appropriateness of those actions to a life that, as they see it, renders everything purposeless. What is appropriate to no goal may be appropriate to goallessness.

Meaning disclaimed

If art may, in the ways just described, disclose meanings, it is natural to speak of art itself possessing meaning in virtue of that capacity. In his classification of the types of meaning possessed by paintings, the art historian Erwin Panofsky includes "intrinsic" meaning. To expose such meaning is to show how, "condensed into [a] work", there is "reveal[ed] the basic attitude of a nation [or] a period" (1970: 55). This is just the kind of "revelation" that Heidegger might expect a "great" work to provide. So Panofsky is recording, with his rather odd label of "intrinsic", that one dimension of an artwork's meaning is precisely its condensation of meanings – those of religious practices, say – discernible in a certain nation or period. Nor, of course, is this the only sort of meaning ascribed to artworks. Panofsky himself lists, in addition, the "factual", "conventional" and "expressional" meanings a painting has when, say, it represents a human being, does so with conventional clues as to his identity (with all those arrows, it must be St Sebastian) and in a manner that expresses deep piety. The list is easily extended. There is the significance a musical phrase has as an appropriate contribution to a whole piece – as a resolution, say, or a bridge. The significance of another phrase may be that it is a quote from a different piece, or a musical joke. Or we may refer to a composition's meaning in virtue of its relationship to other works in a tradition: "Bruckner's Ninth", remarks Wittgenstein, "is a sort of *protest* against Beethoven's" (1980: 34).

One could go on. So the answer to a question raised at the outset of the chapter – whether artworks may have meaning – is a resounding and boring "Yes!" A work may, as George Steiner says (1989: 217), be "brimful of meanings" – ones of as many sorts as there are explanations of meaning and ways of understanding a work or a part of it. Nor, in this connection, should we be overly narrow in what we regard as explanation and understanding. As

MEANING AND THE ARTS 113

Wittgenstein reminds us, "sometimes the simplest explanation [of a musical phrase] is a gesture; on another occasion it might be a dance step, or words describing a dance" (*ibid.*: 69). Each of these, and much else besides, might illuminate the puzzled listener.

Since artworks may so evidently be brimful of meanings, how are we to understand the sentiment famously expressed in Archibald MacLeish's dictum that "A poem should not mean but be"? Similar dicta, ubiquitous these days, are pronounced in relation to other arts: by John Cage, for example, in the case of music, and by almost every Turner Prize hopeful in the case of visual art. ("It were just something to do, like", mumbled one recent winner of the prize). The diagnosis of such disclaimers must, presumably, be that they deny the possibility, importance or value of artworks possessing certain sorts of meaning. For example, in the case of Cage, who wants to "liberate sounds" from the shackles of meaning, the animosity is directed towards the demand that music should have significance in the form of some further, extrinsic purpose. "The highest purpose is to have no purpose at all" (Cage 1968: 155, 159). Contrast Roger Scruton's claim that "meaning in music is a part of aesthetic success" (1993: 194). As it happens, I agree with Scruton; but many do not. Indeed, it is hard to exaggerate how pervasive among contemporary commentators on the arts is the kind of animosity to meaning expressed by Cage. For them, meaning of the sort that vexes them cannot be crucial to an artwork's success, either because it is not something the work can have or because it is incidental to the work's value. Either way, meaning of the kind in question is nothing that the artist should strive for.

While it is absurd to deny *tout court* that artworks possess meaning, disclaimers of particular modes of meaning may be neither mistaken nor uninteresting. In the following sections, I discuss what strike me as the more interesting ones. In the remainder of this section, however, I remark on what strikes me as an unfortunate strategy often followed by disclaimants. This is the strategy of impugning analogies between language and art. It is, the thought goes, only in the case of (prosaic) language that the notion of meaning is clearly defined and understood. To the degree, therefore, that analogies between painting or music and language break down, the extension of the lexicon of meaning to the former is attenuated. (A related strategy, of course, was observed in Chapter 5 among writers loath to deploy the lexicon of meaning in social science.)

One can readily agree that some analogies drawn between language and art have been strained. Talk of vocabularies and grammars of colour or musical sound and of a visual or musical "language of the emotions" is no more promising than the references, noted in Chapter 5, to a semantics and syntax of dress or food. This can be admitted, however, without impugning all of the many analogies between speech and painting or music that have been proposed. Fortunately, I do not need to adjudicate these: my objections to the strategy under consideration do not require defending these analogies. Indeed, my primary objection is this: *so what* if all such analogies fail? That failure would only warrant disclaimers of meaning in art if linguistic meaning – meaning as assigned to words, sentences and their utterances – were privileged over other domains of meaning. I needn't repeat my reasons, given in Chapters 1 and 2, for rejecting such a prioritization. In practice, moreover, those pursuing the strategy I am criticizing tend to focus on only one or two modes of linguistic meaning. They will argue, for example, that linguistic meaning is to be understood in terms of the truth-conditions of sentences, in which event artworks, which allegedly lack truth-conditions, cannot sensibly be spoken of as meaningful – not in a "serious" sense. Again, I won't repeat my reasons for rejecting this further prioritization.

I want also to suggest, without much elaboration, a more subtle objection to the strategy. Its advocates argue, in effect, that our conceptions of linguistic meaning and understanding do not extend to the arts. But there is a particularly pertinent respect in which the conceptions being entertained here may be impoverished. For suppose that understanding of ordinary speech engages, *inter alia*, just those capacities that are exercised in the appreciation of artworks. In that case, the gulf that allegedly separates recognition of linguistic meaning from art appreciation cannot be maintained. And surely that supposition is an attractive one. (In effect, I was defending it in the final section of Chapter 3, when criticizing the "robotic" view of linguistic use and understanding implied by some contemporary accounts of meaning.) Consider two remarks of Wittgenstein's: "There is a strongly musical element in verbal language . . . all the innumerable *gestures* made with the voice"

(1975: §161), and, with reference to a Beethoven movement, "there is something here analogous to the expression of bitter irony in speech" (1980: 55). The first reminds us that, in "the stream of life", understanding what someone is saying requires just the sort of sensitivity to cadence, pauses, emphasis and the like that characterizes appreciation and understanding of music. The second calls our attention to the fact that the use of imagination, the alertness to style and the ability to draw upon a cultural tradition that are at work when we appreciate irony and metaphor are also at work in the understanding of ordinary speech. Only theorists fixated on "Snow is white" or "The cat is on the mat" would fail to recognize that, in "the stream of life", ordinary talk is shot through with metaphor, allusion, irony, hyperbole and much else in the pantheon of rhetoric. What I am suggesting, then, is that *proper* attention to speech, far from impugning the extension to art of the concept of linguistic understanding, would reveal that such understanding is already invested with the very capacities that artists invite their audiences to exercise.

Formalism

Ironically, it is to one perceived parallel between language and art that some important disclaimants of meaning in the latter appeal when articulating their position. Linguists familiarly distinguish between the syntax and semantics of sentences or, more colloquially, between their form and content. Likewise, one may distinguish between the formal aspects of a painting or a song and its content – its subject-matter, say, or its "message". The disclaimants I discuss in this section are those theorists of art often referred to as "formalists", for it is their contention that it is form alone that is the business of art appreciation, either because artworks lack content or because their content is not relevant to their status or value as art. It follows from this contention that modes of meaning which owe to content are outside the scope of art appreciation. Such meanings are either absent from artworks or incidental to them.

Formalist disclaimers are especially familiar from discussions of "pure" music – those of Eduard Hanslick, for example; but they are common as well among visual art critics such as Clive Bell, for whom "significant form" should be the sole preoccupation of critics, who therefore "need bring with [them] nothing from life, no knowledge of its ideas and affairs, no familiarity with its emotions" (1920: 25). Nor are such disclaimers unknown in literary criticism. Maybe MacLeish's dictum was intended to focus our attention, not upon what a poem may be "about", but on such aspects as rhythm and structure. That was certainly the focus of the school of "New Critics" that flourished some decades ago. Indeed, if I devote more space to formalism than some might think it deserves, this is because of the remarkable grip it has exerted on modern aesthetic sensibilities.

In practice, the modes of meaning against which formalists have railed are those of representation and expression. Either artworks don't represent or express anything or, if they do, that is of no moment for their standing and worth. Some formalists have not been especially fastidious in distinguishing between representation and expression – no more, indeed, than everyday speech is: the two terms are, after all, often interchangeable, as in "His gesture represented/expressed hostility". Still, it is useful to heed a distinction between the terms, for they are not everywhere substitutable. A painting, for example, represents – but hardly expresses – a person, thing or event when this is what it refers to or is *of* or *about*. But what if what is represented is an attitude or feeling? Does the painting then express it too? Not necessarily. The reason is that if A expresses B, then A itself has a property described by some expression cognate with "B". A painting, like a face, only expresses sadness if it is sad. Clearly it can be that without referring to or being about sadness. Equally, of course, the painting can represent sadness – be *of* something sad – without itself being sad: it may be a light-hearted piece of *Schadenfreude*.

Formalist denials of representational and expressive meaning to art are variously motivated. The motives range from broadly ideological aims – a desire to elevate "pure" music, for example, or to dissociate the artist, with his purely formal concerns, from dangerous messages that people claim to find in his work (see Goehr 1993) – to reasons of a more technically philosophical kind. Here are two familiar examples. Lurking behind Bell's pronouncement on what the critic need not bring with him is the following thought: since the "aesthetic attitude", as Kant held, is a purely "disinterested" one whereby all concern with what an object (real or represented) is, and since this attitude is the only one that genuinely aesthetic appreciation should cultivate, then such appreciation has no concern with what, if anything, a work represents. The painting may be a portrait of some king, but that is irrelevant to its qualities as a work of art. Secondly, there is the argument that lies behind the following remark of Stravinsky's (which echoes Hanslick): "music is, by its very nature, essentially powerless to *express* anything at all, whether a feeling, an attitude . . . [a] mood . . . etc." (quoted in Sharpe 2000: 56). It is accepted that some music may be provoked by and bear the mark of the composer's emotion, and may in turn "infect" listeners with it; and it is conceded that people may then loosely speak of the music expressing the emotion. But, for Stravinsky and Hanslick, this is indeed loose talk. When we speak of words expressing a feeling, we mean something more than that the words were caused by, and in turn provoke, a feeling. But what could this "more" be in the case of music? Not only does it lack the capacity to register the *thoughts* that particular feelings presuppose (that of danger in the case of fear, say), but the absence of agreement among critics over a piece's expressive content is good evidence that nothing approaching precise correlation obtains between music and emotion or attitude.

This is a book on meaning, not art, and I don't want to become embroiled in issues about the desirability, in general, of artists' striving to achieve meaning through representation and expression. Even less do I want to impugn the tastes of those for whom it is primarily the formal aspects of artworks that they find worth attending to. But it is within the compass of the book to raise certain questions about the formalist approach – questions of cogency, coherence and cost.

To begin with, one may question the cogency of the reasoning that supports formalist conclusions. Certainly the two arguments I mentioned are unimpressive. One might well agree with Bell that the only respectable attitude to take towards artworks is an aesthetic one, rather than, say, a moral, prudential or merely hedonistic one. But it does not follow that the only proper mode of appreciation is the aesthetic one in Kant's particular sense of "disinterestedness". To suppose that someone is abandoning the aesthetic mode the moment he attends to the representational or expressive aspects of a work is bizarre in anything other than that special

sense. Nor, incidentally, was it Kant's own view that art appreciation should be confined to a "disinterested" stance. Indeed, when
he writes that "the poet attempts the task of interpreting to the
sense[s] the rational ideas of invisible beings . . . eternity, creation,
. . . death, envy" and so on (1951: 157), he is all but making explicit
that full appreciation of a poem requires attention to what it com-
municates or means. Nor should we be impressed by Stravinsky's
insistence that music cannot express except in the manner, irrelevant to musical appreciation, of causing or being caused by
feelings, moods or whatever. An analogy with facial expression may
help to make it clear that this is not the only manner of expression.
When, Wittgenstein remarks, we speak of a face expressing
courage, we do not mean that its owner is feeling brave or that it
inspires courage in others. "One might say", rather, that "courage
fits this face" (1969: § 537), though, as his next remark suggests,
one might also say that the face is fitted to – is appropriate to –
courage. Analogously, to call a tune "courageous" or a theme "sad"
is to invoke the normative, not the causal. The tune or theme is
appropriate to the attitude or mood: it fits. That is why we may
agree on understanding it as courageous or sad, why it can communicate something really rather definite to us.

Next one can question the coherence of the formalist position.
Even if it were desirable, is it in fact possible generally to prescind
from attention to representational or expressive aspects of works? I
do not have in mind, primarily, the psychological difficulty of so
prescinding, though it would indeed require an unusual, and
perhaps rather spooky, "mind-set" to look at late Goya or early
Munch paintings in obedience to an instruction to ignore their
representation of twisted limbs or screaming faces, their expression
of agony and *Angst*, and to focus on them merely as formal compo-
sitions. My point, rather, is akin to one made by some linguists
when criticizing others for attempting entirely to divorce syntax
from semantics, form from content. Their point is that the
grammarian would never have lit upon syntactically significant
categories were it not for the contribution to the meanings of
sentences that expressions assigned to these categories generally
make. Admittedly, a certain inflection may not make a regular
semantic contribution and, once identified, may be examined for its
syntactic behaviour alone. But that doesn't alter the fact that, unless

guided by semantic contribution, the inflection would never have been identified as a significant grammatical form. No one, after all, would dream of counting the following sequence of letters in written English – "lve" – as a significant one, despite its cropping up in lots of words ("halve", "salve", "pulverize", etc.). It is the same, I judge, in much art appreciation. Bell is notoriously vague as to how the "significant forms" that are the business of properly aesthetic attention ever get recognized. The answer in the case of many artworks, at least, is surely that these forms are identified in relation to their typical role in representation or expression. Admittedly, in a given painting some blobs of paint that evoke, say, the human body may not, this time, be representing a body. But were it not for the capacity of similar blobs in other paintings to represent the body, it is unclear why these ones should stand out for the viewer's attention – any more than the letters "lve" stand out for the reader's: unclear, that is, what could confer "significant form" upon them.

There is a further, and crucial, point to be made about the coherence or otherwise of formalism. "No composer", observes R. A. Sharpe, "looks more formalistic in his techniques and interests" and ambitions than Schoenberg. Yet, the "power" of his and his followers' music surely "depends on our combining the music with thoughts of the Hapsburg empire, . . . German expressionism" and a whole cultural "milieu a million miles away" from, say, that of seventeenth-century England. Ironically, therefore, our "reception" of such music "gives the lie to the claim that it represents the peak of formalism" (2000: 204–5). I want to generalize and harness Sharpe's observations to make the following point: when an artist aims to eliminate expression from his work, the very attempt to do so – palpable in the work itself – may only serve to confer on it an expressive power that he never intended. *Can* one listen to *Pierrot Lunaire* or stand before a Jackson Pollock without a sense of these works as expressions of distinctively twentieth-century attitudes, anxieties and preoccupations? Well, one could if one was a visiting Martian or someone insulated from any familiarity with that century; but could such a listener or viewer then be intelligently receptive to the power of the works? If not, then he, she or it would be an odd choice as a representative of legitimate art appreciation. It is a great irony that works by Schoenberg and his associates –

composers scornful of any "programme" in music – are, for many listeners, imbued with just the meaning, with just the appropriateness to the troubled Life of the era in which they were written, that other works, like *La Valse*, were intentionally designed to communicate.

Arguably, the point I have extracted from Sharpe is better presented, not as demonstrating the incoherence of formalism, but its cost. Maybe, that is, the point should be that the posture towards art which the formalist enjoins, even if it is one we can adopt, is nothing to celebrate and strive for. As mentioned above, I want to avoid embroilment in issues of taste, in taking sides, for example, over the respective merits of emotionally charged and "cool" art, or of portraiture and "abstract" painting. But it is surely within my remit to make the following brief observation. Human beings are not only, as Merleau-Ponty put it, "condemned" to meaning, as part and parcel of their "being-in-the-world". They are also inveterate searchers for meaning, always on the *qui vive* for meanings beyond those with which they must anyway have traffic in order to comport themselves towards the world and one another. The figures I mentioned at the beginning of this chapter – asking "But what does it mean?" of an apparently senseless installation or musical piece – are, one might say, being "only human". They are not naïve relics of a bygone culture, not yet inducted into the sophistication of a modern art world; rather, they are registering the abiding concern for significance of which art itself, for millennia, has been a striking manifestation. If contemporary culture is able to accommodate formalism, this is, I suspect, only because the works and attitudes it favours themselves become fodder for the very concerns about meaning that formalism aims to consign to the past.

I leave the final word to Ronald Hepburn when remarking on the cost of what he calls "the objectivizing way". He has in mind those who advocate looking at the natural world only in the objective manner of the scientist. But his verdict is equally applicable to those who advocate an exclusively formalist approach to art. That approach sacrifices "intentional density": it is a "kind of spiritual suicide through the attenuation of all the aspects of our dealings with the world [and art] that involve the acknowledgement of meaning" (2001: 30–31). That is the "cost" of formalism, and a high one.

"The role of the reader"

I have not, since the chapter's opening paragraph, mentioned the issue about meaning and art over which most ink has been spilled in recent times, mainly by literary critics, though the issue is by no means confined to literature. What has been disclaimed by many of these critics is that the author's or artist's meaning or intention can settle understanding and interpretation of his creations: either such intentions cannot be identified or they are anyway irrelevant to interpretation of works. This disclaimer need not go with a wider disclaimer of meaning in art, but it often does. The larger thought it inspires is that artworks do not *have* meanings; rather these are conferred or "projected" by audiences. It is a thought encapsulated in Roland Barthes' slogan, "the death of the author is the birth of the reader" (1977: 148). What the artist cannot fix, different audiences can variously confer. This demotic principle is today's fashionable retort to John Ruskin's stentorian injunction to "be sure that you go to the author to get at *his* meaning, not to find yours" (1903–12: I §13).

Identification of what is at issue here – between, say, Ruskin and Barthes – has been occluded by two unfortunate tendencies in modern debates. The first is the prominence in those debates – English-language ones, at least – of a heavily anthologized article by Beardsley and Wimsatt (1976), "The Intentional Fallacy". This is often taken as the seminal text for the rejection of any equation between a work's meaning and the intention of its maker. The trouble is that this is not, in fact, what is rejected in their article. All that they try to show is that intentions *other than* those which, so to speak, may be read off from the works themselves – ones, for example, that we only glean from diaries or TV interviews – are not germane to interpretation. Indeed, when they write that "if the poet succeeded . . . then the poem itself shows what he was trying to do" and the "the question about intention" is thereby answered, they themselves seem actually to identify the meaning of the poem with the relevant intention of the poet (1976: 4. For this point, see Lyas 1997: Ch. 8).

A second unfortunate tendency, exhibited by Beardsley and Wimsatt among others, is to treat it as a straightforward matter of fact whether or not authorial intention settles the question of a work's meaning. But, of course, whether reference to intention does this depends on what the questioner was asking. In some contexts, as we saw in Chapter 2, what he is requesting when asking "What does this mean?" may be precisely an indication of what a speaker, author or artist intended to achieve or communicate. It is silly, then, to register one's hostility towards concern with artists' intentions by saying that it is a *mistake* ever to identify meanings with intentions. (When, in Chapter 4, I criticized the "Gricean programme" for reducing word- and sentence-meaning to speakers' meanings or intentions, the point was not to deny that, on occasions, the appropriate and apposite explanation of a word's meaning will refer us to such intentions, but to insist that, in other contexts, that is not the kind of explanation that is wanted.)

So how should we construe the issue? Is there, in fact, a real issue at all? Can't it be settled by getting the contestants to agree that indication of an artist's intention is one respectable way of explaining a work's meaning, but by no means the only way? From one angle of interest, what Eliot intended to communicate by "I will show you fear in a handful of dust" determines the line's meaning; from other angles, it doesn't. This way of settling the issue might seem congenial to the catholic approach to meaning encouraged in the present book, with its stress on the many different respects in which meaning is attributed. Matters cannot be left here, however, for there are real issues at stake, albeit ones that modulate into large disputes about the role of art that are outside the compass of a book on meaning. What is at issue, surely, is the value and cost in the reception of artworks of, respectively, focusing exclusively upon and ignoring artists' intentions.

I shall approach the issue by remarking on something already illustrated by the Eliot line – something that is both an analogy with art and, very often, an important ingredient in art; namely, metaphor. I use the term in a wide way: as the name, first, for a whole range of traditional tropes (metonymy, synecdoche etc.) and not just for metaphors in contrast with these; secondly, for what whole literary works, not just particular lines, might exhibit (*Animal Farm*, for example, as a metaphor for Soviet Russia); and, finally, for what non-verbal works may also contain or be (if Romeo can metaphorically describe Juliet as the sun, a cartoonist may metaphorically depict her as such). In one respect, however, I use the term more narrowly than it often is: I am only concerned with "live" or "creative" metaphors, not with "dead" or "conventional" ones, like "My husband was a pig". (The distinction, of course, is not a sharp one.)

A comparison of metaphors with artworks is important for our purposes, because the question raised about the relevance of their creators' intentions to the meanings of the latter is one that has also been raised about the relevance of intentions to metaphorical meaning. In particular, there corresponds to the claim, with respect to literary works, that "a determinate meaning requires a determining will" (Hirsch 1967: 266) the claim that the metaphorical meaning of an utterance is fixed by what the speaker intended to convey (see Searle 1979: 76–116). To recognize the weaknesses in, or intolerable one-sidedness of, that second claim – an application of one of the strait-jacketing accounts of linguistic meaning discussed in Chapters 2 and 3 – will enable us to appreciate the legitimacy of complaints against the first.

There are many weaknesses in the claim that understanding a metaphor is necessarily a matter of discerning the speaker's communicative intention (even in those lucky cases where we know who the speaker was). Two are especially germane to the present discussion. First the intentionalist claim implies that, where we do know what the speaker intended, it must just be wrong to interpret the metaphor except on the basis of that intention. But this is not at all, in practice, how we generally respond to metaphors. Suppose we discovered, from a diary or letter, that when Shakespeare spoke of music as the food of love, he intended to communicate that sheet-music, when eaten, acts as an aphrodisiac. I doubt that literary critics or anyone else would then feel obliged to take the metaphor in that way. Secondly, the intentionalist claim makes it difficult to see why people should ever speak metaphorically: by holding that the metaphorical speaker is indirectly communicating a proposition other than the one his words literally mean, it is implied that he could have communicated the same by a direct, literal utterance of the intended proposition instead. Indeed, metaphorical talk would be perverse: why put hearers to the effort of "decoding" a message that could have been communicated "straight"?

These criticisms prompt the following reflections on metaphor. First, a metaphor, once introduced, becomes public property: it is, as Derrida nicely puts it, abandoned to its own "drift . . . orphaned and separated since birth from the support of [its] father" (1982: 316). How people receive and use the metaphor is not dictated by its "father's" will, even if it is clear what that was. To be sure, someone might, whenever encountering metaphor, confine his efforts to searching for the proposition intended by its maker, but this would be unusual. To begin with, if that were the general response to metaphor, it is unclear why it would ever be produced: speakers would simply "tell it straight", without putting their listeners through an interpretative detour. Secondly, it is quite wrong to think that, at all generally, the appropriate response to a metaphor is to seek some proposition communicated by the speaker. Typically, the force of a metaphor is to evoke imagery, to prompt novel lines of thought, to suggest a new vocabulary for talking about something, or to intimate a way of "seeing as". A really good metaphor, like "Architecture is frozen music", does all of these.

This point is very persuasively argued by Davidson in "What Metaphors Mean" (in Davidson 1984). He goes on, however, to draw the unnecessarily paradoxical conclusion that metaphors do not mean at all. At one time (Cooper 1986), I followed him here; but, as the present book will have made clear, I no longer see reason to think that the meaning of a sentence is something that is only indicated by referring to some associated proposition or set of truth-conditions. (Davidson's conclusion relies on the thoughts that meaning is to be indicated by truth-conditions and that (fresh) metaphors do not have such conditions.) By indicating the imagery evoked by a metaphor, the lines of thought it opens up and so on, what one is doing, surely, is to explain one's understanding of the metaphor and how one takes it to mean.

A final point is that what the speaker intended by his metaphor might be so much less interesting than other interpretations it invites. Why, then, be constrained by that intention? Certainly it is our practice with metaphor *not* to be so constrained. (Recall the example of Shakespeare's imagined intention behind "if music be the food of love".)

Interpreting a metaphor, I want to say, is a matter of appropriating it and putting it to work – the work, *inter alia*, of stimulating the imagination and suggesting fruitful models for conceptualizing something. Something like a "principle of charity" informs the interpretation of metaphor: we try to make the best out of metaphors, to render them maximally appropriate to our imaginative and intellectual endeavours. That is why, typically, the intention of their makers is not "the last word". That intention may give us too "thin" a reading of the metaphor, one that dilutes the "density", to recall Hepburn's term, of the metaphor.

In all of this, surely, there is an analogy with understanding the meaning of an artwork. Indeed, as noted above, a work may in effect *be* a metaphor. To invert Paul Ricoeur's observation that a metaphor is "a poem in miniature" (1977: 94), some poems are jumbo-sized metaphors. To be sure, there are people whose interest in artworks is really confined to ar*tists*: those, for example, who stand before a Picasso preoccupied by whether he was aiming to convey his love or loathing of some ex-mistress portrayed on the canvas. This, however, is but one, not especially laudable or central, way of concerning oneself with a work. It is not, as some disclaimants of intended meaning state, a mistake to indicate the meaning of a poem or painting by referring to its creator's intention. That is something we can and sometimes want to do. Their real point, I think, is that there are weightier and loftier concerns to have about an artwork, ones that prompt very different styles or modes of indicating meaning. These will be the modes we employ when, for example, articulating the flight of imagination provoked by a work, its capacity to encapsulate a new way of thinking about human relationships and its revelation – in the sense discussed earlier in the chapter – of the otherwise inconspicuous significance of certain things. To interpret a work and explain its meaning in these ways is to indicate its versatile modes of appropriateness; and since the use of imagination, the ongoing attempt to conceptualize human relationships and our traffic with a world of significance are all crucial dimensions of our form of life, interpretation must also aspire to indicate art's appropriateness to Life itself.

7 The meaning of life

The eponymous heroine of Michael Ondaatje's *Anil's Ghost* is disillusioned, no longer able to "believe that meaning allowed a person a door to escape grief and fear" (2000: 55). It is a belief, however, that most of us are reluctant to abandon. A typical response, after all, by those whom tragedy affects – the loss of a child, say – is to seek some "sense to it" that might redeem the event from sheer pointless contingency. It is not, of course, only in order to confront grief and fear that people seek meaning or sense in their intercourse with the world. Human beings are inveterately teleological beings: they are not, as I remarked in Chapter 6, merely "condemned" as beings-in-the-world to traffic with meanings, but always on the *qui vive* for further meanings that lend sense and point to their activities. Nietzsche only moderately exaggerates when observing that "if you have your *why?* for life, you can get along with almost any *how?*" (1954: maxim 12). It might indeed strike a visiting alien that it matters less to people how they spend their time than that, whatever this is, it is something that affords meaning, in their eyes, to their occupations.

It is unsurprising, in the light of this, that people proceed to ask questions, not about the significance of this or that activity or event, but about the significance of human life itself. Indeed, perhaps this procession is inevitable. To enquire into an item's meaning, I urged in Chapter 2, is to enquire into its connection with something outside or larger than itself. But this latter is likely, in its turn, to be an item whose meaning is in question. Indeed, unless it can be seen as meaningful, it would seem incapable of conferring meaning on the item originally enquired into. Arguably, we must proceed or ascend to seeking meaning in human life itself as the something in connection with which any action or practice has significance. For if that turns out to be "a tale told by an idiot . . . signifying nothing", can anything that belongs to or participates in it be meaningful? As Robert Nozick puts it, when it comes to how we live our days, "we want meaning all the way down. Nothing less will do" (1981: 599).

Before I plunge into the issues posed by these observations – into whether it is sensible to ask for the meaning of life and, if it is, what modes of response are available – some further preliminary remarks, of a methodological character, might prove helpful.

A sensible question?

In this section, I begin with those further remarks and then consider some familiar reasons for impatience with the question of the meaning of life. (Rumour has it that a main motive for making formal logic a compulsory first-year course at Oxford was to disabuse students of their image of philosophy as preoccupied with the meaning of life.)

Even if the question "What is the meaning of life?" were a sensible one and I knew the answer to it, it would not be my aim in this chapter to supply that answer. That task no more belongs to a book about meaning in general than does supplying an answer to the question "What is the meaning of that poem?" – a job, surely, for the poet, the literary critic or sensitive reader. In Chapter 6, certainly, I wrote about the meaning of poems but, so to speak, at a "meta" level; my concern there was not with the meanings of particular poems, but with the modes of meaning that poems might sensibly be said to possess. Philosophical enquiry into meaning, I remarked in Chapter 1, is into the meaning of meaning: not only, I added, into the meaning of the word "meaning", but into the import, function and status of the notion of meaning. In keeping with that conception, our present enquiry is not intended to furnish the right answer – God? The goal of history? The meaning *we* give it? The Absolute? The number 42? – to "What is the meaning of life?", but to explore the notion of life's having a meaning and to reflect on what, if anything, could count as suitable explanations or indications of life's meaning.

The character of this enquiry implies a restriction that is worth making explicit. I shall, in fact, be defending the notion of the meaning of life, but only against a certain sort of critic. "The truth was", so Tolstoy summarized his reflections in *My Confession*, "that life was meaninglessness". This is because we are mortal. "Is there in my life", he rhetorically asks, "a meaning which would not be destroyed by my . . . death?" (in Hanfling 1987: 11, 14). That I will die – that, indeed, the human race will disappear – renders senseless all the deeds, such as writing *War and Peace*, to which we are prone to ascribe significance. Tolstoy is, in effect, conceding that life might have had meaning, for we might have been immortals. It's just that the relevant condition is not satisfied. It is *not* with such deniers of the meaning of life that I want to cross swords. I am concerned, not with whether what would make life meaningful actually obtains, but with whether there is anything that could make life meaningful. My adversaries, whom we will soon meet, are those for whom there is something wrong with the very idea of the meaning of life, for whom it is a mistake even to ask what it is.

My second methodological remark also concerns the scope of the enquiry. What do we have in mind by life when we enquire into its meaning or lack of one? Are we speaking of individual human lives or of Life, the human "form of life" or "Life-world" into which my life and your life are woven? It is possible for someone to hold that both Life and his life are meaningful; that Life is meaningful, but his isn't; that Life has no meaning, but a particular life, like his, does; or that neither Life nor his life is meaningful. The third view, for example, might be that of someone who thinks that his life has the meaning *he* gives to it, but that Life is without an owner or subject to confer meaning upon it. The second view might be taken by a person who thinks that, while Life as a whole has meaning (a divine purpose, say), his own life (disowned, perhaps, by God) fails to share in it. My attention will be to Life. This is partly because I think it is the question of Life's meaning that has most concerned people. (For Tolstoy, it is not simply *his* death, but the coming to an end of Life, that renders everything senseless. If Life had meaning – because it was eternal – his own life could participate in it.) But it is partly, as well, because the idea of Life's having meaning is the most philosophically problematic. At any rate, it is the one which has most attracted the sceptical or dismissive attitudes to which I shortly turn.

In attending to Life, rather than to my life or yours, I do not, of course, deny the importance of questions concerning the meaning of an individual life. Nor do I deny that meaning may, on a variety of grounds and from several angles of concern, be properly attributed to an individual life. Perhaps it is a life that contributes to a further and noble social end; or one with a marked "narrative structure", so that it "hangs together", its parts coherently related in the manner of the episodes in a well-wrought novel; or one that is not badly out of kilter with, and hence inappropriate to, the age in which it is lived; or one whose central "projects" leave their trace and are not self-defeating. (Bartlebooth, in Georges Perec's *Life: a User's Manual*, resolves that "his whole life would be organized around a single project . . . with no purpose outside of its own completion . . . no trace" (1988: 117–19). One can understand the judgement that such a life is without meaning, especially when, in Bartlebooth's case, the project – to solve jigsaw puzzles – ends with him dying while holding a piece that won't fit into the only remaining space.) Indeed, it is partly because it is so easy to specify respects in which an individual life may be judged meaningful or otherwise that the more problematic philosophical issue is the one concerned with Life.

Among the sceptical or dismissive attitudes to the idea of Life's meaning, one should first distinguish between those which involve blunt rejection of the question of Life's meaning and those which, rather more gently, view it as an unfortunate formulation of questions that are not really about meaning at all. Let's begin with these latter. The thought is that when people ask "What is the meaning of Life?", they are raising any of several questions that could be paraphrased, to the same people's satisfaction, by ones that do not invoke a vocabulary of meaning. Perhaps what is being asked is, for example, whether Life has any value, or whether Life is progressing to some final state, or whether there is any explanation of why Life has come to be what it is. Such questions may or may not be sensible and answerable, but even if they are, it would be misleading to proclaim that Life therefore has a meaning. Instead one should more soberly conclude, for example, that yes, we can see Life as progressing towards a certain state.

The diagnosis, on which the above strategy relies, of what people intend when they ask about Life's meaning is, however, a poor one. Granted, they may well be concerned to know what value there is to Life, whether it is approaching a final state, or what may explain it. Not just any old value, state or explanation, however, is what they are after, but only one of a type capable of conferring meaning. I cannot imagine many people thinking that their question "Has Life a meaning?" has received an affirmative answer on being informed, say, that Life has value *qua* a contribution to ecological stability or because, on some hedonic calculus, the sum total of utility exceeds that of disutility in the history of Life. Nor, surely, would some naturalistic, evolutionary tale that explains why the human form of life has emerged as it has be seen as providing an affirmative answer. Such values or explanations are the wrong sort. Indeed, I suspect the very opposite to the proposed diagnosis is closer to the truth: when people ask "Does Life have a value?" or "Why are we here and where are we going?", their questions are, implicitly, ones about the meaning of Life. Far from it being the case that these latter invite paraphrase into the former, the paraphrasing must go in the other direction if the questioners' intent is to be properly diagnosed. The value, whence and whither that they seek should be of a kind that confers meaning on Life.

Let me now turn to blunter dismissals of the question. In their most common form, these will be of a kind familiar to readers of Chapters 5 and 6. There, the tactic of those who disclaimed use of the vocabulary of meaning in the domains of social science and art criticism was, typically, to emphasize differences between these domains and that of language, allegedly the paradigmatic domain of meaning. Recall, for example, the claim that symbolic behaviour is too unlike verbal utterance for the notion of meaning to get a grip on it. Or recall the claim that music, while it possesses something like a "syntax", lacks the "semantic content" that linguistic performances have. In the present context, and at its crudest, the charge is that, since only words, sentences, utterances and what are closely analogous to these can sensibly be said to possess meaning, it is nonsense to speak of Life having meaning. It is, after all, neither a linguistic item nor remotely analogous to one. Since the assumption that meaning is confined within the linguistic domain is absurd, this form of dismissal need not be taken seriously.

There is, however, a less crude form of dismissal, one that this time invokes an alleged parallel with language. What gets dismissed is the line of thought that, I suggested at the beginning of the chapter, generates the question of the meaning of Life: the thought that, for anything we do to be meaningful, meaning must go "all the way down", to Life itself. If Life itself is without meaning, does meaning not leach out from everything? That thought, it is charged, is a bad one, as reflection on a parallel with language quickly reveals. Words and sentences, it is argued (on Saussurean or Davidsonian lines), have meaning only in virtue of their relation to a language as a whole. But the question "And so what is the meaning of that language as a whole – French, say?" sounds silly. It is therefore clear, the reasoning goes, that what enables linguistic items to have meaning need not itself have meaning. It's the same with Life. Practices, ambitions, projects and achievements have their significance through their place in, contribution or other connection to Life. It doesn't follow that Life itself must have meaning; indeed, the analogy with language should encourage us to resist such an attribution.

I don't, for the moment, want to defend the "all the way down" line of thought against which the above argument is directed. I do, however, want to challenge the analogy with language on which the argument relied – or, rather, to propose a more apposite one that does not yield the same dismissive conclusion. Since it is a concern with what we *do* – our actions, practices and so forth – that generates the question of the meaning of Life, the apposite analogy would be, not with the words and sentences of a language, but with the *uses* of these, with "speech acts". Now these, too, depend for their significance on a vast complex of linguistic behaviour. But whereas it was silly to ask for the meaning of the French language considered as a *langue* – a reservoir of words, grammatical devices and so on – it is not similarly immediately silly to ask for the meaning of language as *parole*, for the significance of our engagement in linguistic behaviour. Indeed, given that the human form of life is indelibly that of language-users, to ask for the meaning of Life *is*, in important part, to ask what meaning there may be to a Life unimaginable in abstraction from the dedication of its participants to *parole*. If the question, so construed, of the meaning of language as such turns out to be silly, this will be because the question of the meaning of Life is wrong-headed – not vice versa.

Appropriateness, Life and God

That the analogy on which the foregoing dismissal of the "all the way down" line of thought rested was a poor one does not entail, however, that the line of thought is unproblematic. The difficulty with it is best articulated in the terminology of appropriateness. Items are meaningful, I have been suggesting throughout this book, in virtue of their appropriateness to something larger than or outside themselves. Ultimately, I also argued, it is to Life itself that they are appropriate, even if it is rarely the case that, in indicating or explaining meanings, it is necessary explicitly to invoke that final terminus. But now it should be clear why it is problematic to speak of Life as meaningful. To what could it, as the terminus or background to all explanations of appropriateness, itself be appropriate? As Dilthey put it, "Life is the fundamental fact . . . behind which it is impossible to go" (1923–: VII 359). Life, he writes elsewhere, is self-enclosed. While, like the notes that contribute to a whole melody, particular actions may be meaningful through contributing to Life, Life itself, like the melody, "expresses nothing but itself" (1979: 237).

What options are available, in the face of this difficulty, to someone sympathetic to the notion of Life's meaning? Rejection or amendment, it would seem, of at least one of the following claims: (a) Life is the terminus "behind which it is impossible to go", and (b) the meaning of something is appropriateness to what is larger than or outside itself. For if Life is meaningful then, by (b), it relates to what is beyond itself, in which case (a) cannot be maintained.

Let's begin by considering two attempts to secure the meaningfulness of Life by jettisoning (b). The first – reminiscent of Aquinas's doctrine of "analogical predication" – invokes a distinction between a "primary" and a "secondary" sense of "meaningful". Consider the word "healthy". This, let's assume, primarily applies to whatever promotes a long and disease-free life. Eating your greens, exercising, fresh air and a steady pulse are healthy in this sense. But we also speak of a healthy life. In this "secondary" or "analogical" sense, "healthy" cannot mean what contributes to a life; rather, it refers to a life that is full of healthy (primary sense) ingredients – the life of someone who eats his greens, exercises and so on. Similarly, it is argued, to refer to Life as meaningful is to use the adjective in a secondary sense: it indicates that Life is full of actions, practices, projects and so on that are meaningful in the primary sense of being appropriate to Life. There is no need, then, to suppose that, in order to count as meaningful, Life must connect with something beyond itself.

In response to this first attempt, one need not deny that it captures what someone might intend by saying that Life is meaningful. One thinks of references, by Heidegger and others, to our human world as a —"totality of significance". But, as I argued earlier in the chapter, it does not capture what people who ask for the meaning of Life are normally seeking. That Life is meaningful in the sense of being replete with activities, such as uttering sentences, doffing one's cap and working for "a good cause", that have meaning, is hardly in dispute. To point it out, therefore, can do nothing to satisfy the urge to look for meaning "all the way down". The point is compatible, after all, with regarding Life as a senseless contingency, an idiot's tale, a self-stultifying Schopenhauerian oscillation between frustrated desire and boredom, a plaything of a whimsical god, a "nothingness" confronted in Heideggerian *Angst* and as any number of other possibilities which, if realized, would persuade most people that Life has no meaning. The point does nothing to allay, therefore, the feeling that, unless Life has meaning in the "primary" sense, the appropriateness to Life of our activities is not worth the candle – to allay, that is, the feeling that significance leaches out from those activities, which now become as pointless, empty or frivolous as what they contribute to.

A second attempt to secure the meaningfulness of Life by dropping (b) goes like this. Meaning is indeed appropriateness to Life; but that only rules out speaking of Life itself as having meaning, however, if appropriateness is taken to be an irreflexive relation – one that something cannot stand in to itself. But why accept that assumption? Why should Life not be appropriate to itself, rather than to something larger than or outside it? In other words, why should Life not be its own meaning? Maybe this was Dilthey's thought when he remarked that Life "expresses nothing but itself".

I agree with Nozick (1981: 600ff.) that the idea of something being its own meaning should not be dismissed "just like that", paradoxical as it might sound. (The case he discusses is *Ein Sof*, the "unlimited" in Jewish mystical thought.) One can, at any rate, think of considerations that might motivate the idea. For example, a Hegelian distinction between the "actual" and the "real", with the implied possibility that how something actually is may not be appropriate to or fully realize how it "really" or essentially is. Or again, the not unattractive thought might be that X is its own meaning when the urge to keep pressing Tolstoy's question, "And then what?", is stilled by recognition of X – when, as it were, appreciation of X brings peace to those who have been pressing the questions, one after another, of the form "And what does *that* mean?".

I shall return to this latter consideration in the next section. For the moment, I remark that, even if there is mileage in the thought of something's being its own meaning, Life does not appear to be a plausible candidate for that distinction. Self-evidently, people do experience an urge to ask "And then what?" of Life itself: recognition of Life, therefore, cannot still the urge to press that question, cannot bring peace. Indeed, it is hard to hear "Life is its own meaning" or "Life is appropriate to itself" as more than an impatient way of exhorting people to stop agonizing over Life's meaning – as, in effect, denying rather than endorsing the notion of Life's meaning.

Let's turn now, then, to the attempt to secure that notion which involves rejection of (a) – the claim that Life is the terminus, "behind" or "beyond" which it is illegitimate to look for a source of meaning. There can be no doubt as to which version of this attempt has been most popular. It is God who stands behind Life, and God's purpose that stands beyond the confines of Life. As one critic of this view explains it, just as an individual's life is called meaningful if it helps in "the realization of some plan or purpose transcending his own concerns", so the Life of man is "guaranteed significance by the knowledge that he is participating in God's purpose" (Baier 1987: 23–4). Certainly many of those who deny, cheerfully or otherwise, that Life has meaning do so on the grounds that it has no such "outside" purpose.

As noted in earlier chapters, to ask for something's meaning is, in some contexts, to ask what end or purpose it is appropriate to. Hence, to explain how something is appropriate to some purpose is a perfectly respectable mode of meaning-indication. Should we straightaway conclude, then, that if there is a divine purpose to which Life suitably contributes, the answer to the question of whether Life has a meaning is a resounding affirmative? That conclusion would be far too hasty: the question of Life's meaning that is being addressed in this chapter is not at all equivalent to that of whether Life contributes to a purpose, divine or otherwise. This can be appreciated as soon as we reflect that the admission of certain contributions and purposes would certainly not persuade the questioner that Life therefore has meaning.

To begin with, one can imagine divine plans in which the role of Life is too instrumental or modest to confer meaning on it: its Gaia-like contribution, say, to maintaining chemical equilibrium in one tiny part of the universe, or its serving as a brief and necessary bridge between the apes and the robots. Or one can imagine divine purposes too mad, Machiavellian or frivolous to confer meaning on Life. Maybe God created us so that he might enjoy the spectacle of creatures tortured by the question of why he created them. Or maybe he created the world as a mere toy, a gigantic dolls' house whose inhabitants it occasionally amuses him to move around. So not just any old purpose or contribution will do. Nor, arguably, will those purposes and contributions that theologians have often identified. Consider, for example, the claim – popular in Christian and Islamic theology – that God created Life so that he might see himself reflected in his human creatures and/or be loved by these creatures. It might surely and sensibly be asked what the point or sense of such a purpose could be, and if that question receives no satisfactory answer, it is unclear how this purpose redeems Life from meaninglessness. After all, if I genetically engineer some clones to reflect and admire me, that hardly settles the meaningfulness of their and my existence. Why should it be different simply because the engineer is God?

One can go further. Plans and purposes, even when they are God's, are the wrong type of items to serve as termini to questions of the form "And what is the meaning of *that*?" The issue recalls the one raised in Plato's dialogue, *Euthyphro*. There the issue, put in modern dress, was whether something is good because the gods will it or whether, instead, the gods will it because it is good. The present issue is whether Life is meaningful because it is appropriate to some divine plan or whether God decided on that plan because it incorporated a meaningful form of human Life. The first disjunct, I have argued, must be rejected: meaning is not guaranteed by God's having a purpose to which Life contributes. The second disjunct presupposes that there is a standard by which to judge Life meaningful that is independent of God's purpose. God's decision to create Life as it is will have been shaped, in part at least, by his prior recognition of its being a meaningful one. But in that case, the appeal to God's purpose or plan has got us nowhere in understanding what, if anything, renders Life meaningful. God's purpose will explain why there *is* meaningful Life, since he created it, but not why that Life is meaningful.

Limitlessness

In the preceding section, I rehearsed the options available to someone sympathetic to the idea of the meaning of Life in the face of the obvious problem, concerning the "all the way down" line of thought, described at the beginning of the section. Neither option, however, seemed to work out. Life could not provide itself with meaning, and moving to what is outside Life – to God's plan – took us nowhere. Doubtless it is the failure of these options that has convinced many philosophers that the question of Life's meaning should be buried. The trouble is it won't stay buried. It is apparent that very many people find intolerable the idea that Life is without meaning, not least because of its nihilistic impact, as they experience it, on the meaningfulness of their own particular lives. Such people may indeed be unable to state what the meaning of Life is: maybe, they concede, it is a mystery – but something mysterious is better than nothing at all.

I am deeply sympathetic to this attitude. Not only do I find it impossible to bury the question, but I shall be defending the thought that, if there is meaning to Life, it not only *is*, but *must be*, mysterious. To prepare for that defence, I will need both to recall some prior themes (including the rejection of "objectivist" accounts of meaning in Chapter 4) and to revise the terms in which, so far, I have been addressing the question.

I want to recall, first, my brief mention, in the previous section, of the thoughts that what gives Life meaning would have to be its own meaning and that this source would have to be the "limitless", "inexhaustible" or "encompassing", to cite Nozick's, Gabriel

Marcel's and Karl Jaspers's expressions. The first thought, I implied, might be taken as gesturing towards the idea of the source of meaning as that which, when recognized, simply stills the urge to ask, yet again, "And then what?" Or, as Marcel puts it, of this source we must be able to say "There is no more", but not, this time, in a mood of despair or frustration ("Is *that* all there is?!") – rather, in peace and satisfaction (Marcel 1949: 69). It was the second thought, however, that seemed to rule out Life itself as a candidate for self-meaning. Life, as it were, is too small – not sufficiently "encompassing" or "limitless" – to serve as the terminus of the series of "And then what?" questions. Size matters – which is why the search was on for something larger than or outside Life as the source of its meaning.

What I now want to suggest is that the terms in which we have been speaking – in particular of what is "larger than" or "outside" Life – have been misleading. When talking, in earlier chapters, of the meanings of words, gestures, artworks, symbols or whatever, that terminology was harmless and helpful. It was not difficult, for example, to understand how a word's meaning could be indicated in terms of its contribution to larger linguistic items, notably sentences. Again, one could grasp without trouble the idea of an artwork having a meaning through representing or expressing something outside itself. When one turns to Life, however, this spatial rhetoric becomes problematic. It does, at any rate, if one accepts the position I recommended in Chapter 4.

In Chapter 4, meaning-scepticism was not bluntly rejected, but "tamed" by treating it as an exaggerated and misleading statement of an "anti-realist" or "anti-objectivist" account of meaning that I then proceeded to defend. What words apply to, and so mean, is not determined independently of "ongoing use and ratification", of "moves in a sort of life", of human perspectives and interests. This account, I suggested, belonged to a wider or global anti-objectivism. If it applies to words, it also applies to the things that words speak of. For things, too, are meaningful items, owing their identity to their place in that "referential totality" that is the world. The world as we describe it is not what is there anyway, already sliced at joints corresponding to our articulation of it. It is a "human world", as phenomenologists say, no more independent from Life than are the meanings of words.

If this suggestion is plausible, then the rhetoric of what is larger than or outside Life is an unhappy one. For what is suggested, one is tempted to say, is that there is nothing of which we can speak that is larger than or outside Life, for nothing of which we can speak is independent of Life. But that way of talking can itself mislead, conjuring up an idealist vision of the world somehow being contained within Life. (Think of the fate, among impatient and unsympathetic critics, of Derrida's claim – not a million miles away from mine – that "there is no outside-of-the-text".) Rather than resist that temptation, however, I exhort readers to dispel the misleading vision and instead to read the remark that nothing articulatable is larger than or outside Life as stating, simply, that no articulation of the world can pretend to describe the world as it anyway is, independently of the moves, perspectives, practices and interests that belong to Life.

Several of those readers, I suspect, are now expecting me to draw the following conclusion from this discussion. Life *is*, after all, "big" enough – sufficiently unlimited and encompassing – to be its own meaning, the terminus that stills the quest for meaning and brings peace. Beyond Life, we can say, "there is no more" but no longer, as it were, out of the frustration or despair of someone who reasonably expected that there would be more. What made Life seem an unpromising candidate for terminal self-meaning was the assumption that it was limited, that there was something further than or outside it, something it might be, or fail to be, appropriate to. With that assumption rejected, there is no reason not to regard Life as the sole source of meaning – of the meanings of everything that is appropriate to it and, in the special sense indicated, of itself.

This conclusion, which it would not have been unreasonable of readers to predict, is not, however, the one I want to draw. Why I don't is the topic of the following and final section.

Mystery and measure

While the predicted conclusion is not my own, nor is it one that I would cavalierly dismiss. At the end of the day, perhaps, the test of whether an answer to the question of Life's meaning is a satisfying one is whether it does in fact satisfy people by stilling their urge to keep pressing the question. And perhaps there are people who would find satisfying the proposal that a Life no longer conceived of as limited by anything "outside" it is its own meaning. (Maybe they are people impressed, in their romantic youth, by Hegelian speculations of a self-realizing, all-encompassing *Geist* that is the source of all meaning, and who now find in Life a more tractable, less "metaphysical" substitute for *Geist*.)

I suspect, however, that there are not many such people, for a reason that concerns an aspect of the quest for Life's meaning that I have not yet made explicit. Marcel speaks of a "humility" which is the antithesis of a hubris that "consists in drawing strength solely from [ourselves]", and which recognizes that something "has a hold over me" to which I should "respond" (1948: 20 and 1949: 46). The disquiet, I suggest, that does much to drive the quest for Life's meaning is precisely the fear that nothing "has a hold over" Life, that there is nothing beyond it for it to "respond" to. Such disquiet registers a need to suppose that there is a measure of Life, something for it to be answerable to. For if there is not – if all measure is provided from within Life, by the practices, projects and conventions that human beings happen to have devised for themselves – there is no preventing the corrosive conviction that nothing we do is, finally, of significance. Had Life gone differently, we would have been doing different things, and how, in the absence of measure, could we think that this would matter? And if it wouldn't matter, how can it matter either that we are doing what we in fact do?

The idea of a measure of Life, however, seems to take us back a step – to the rejected thought of a world outside Life. But this is not so, and for a reason that returns me to my remark (p. 136) about the mysteriousness of Life's meaning. When denying, in the last section, that there is a world outside Life, I was careful to specify that, by "world", I meant an articulatable, describable world. My claim, recall, was that this world is not independent of Life, is not what there anyway is. Given this, there is available, at least as a formal option, the following possibility: there is indeed a "beyond the human", a "beyond Life", but this is necessarily mysterious, since it cannot be described or articulated. Available, too, is the further possibility that it is precisely this mysterious "beyond" that may confer meaning on Life, for it may provide measure and be what Life is answerable to. So the idea of measure need not return us to the discredited, "objectivist" notion of an articulatable world outside Life.

This will all be too heady for some people, but it is important to emphasize that the position is not an idiosyncratic one of my own. On the contrary, the vision of an ineffable reality that provides a measure of Life is ancient and pervasive. One thinks of the Tao or Way that, while it may not be spoken of, is the Way that gives measure to human ways. Or of an ineffable "Emptiness" to which, in some Buddhist traditions, our lives should be attuned. It is a vision shared, in recent times, by Marcel, who speaks of a "principle of inexhaustibility", Being, which we should, in a "sense of stewardship", hold ourselves "responsible towards" (1949: 102). Heidegger, too, writes of that mysterious well-spring, Being, from which comes "the assignment of those directives that must become law and rule for man" (1993: 262).

In another work, I defend at some length both the idea of mystery and the claim that, in what is mysterious, there is a measure of Life that, despite the ineffability of what is mysterious, we may hope to discern (Cooper 2002: Chs 10–13). If Life is without meaning, it is because it *fails* to measure up, not because it is without measure. I cannot provide that defence here, so I must content myself with the conditional claim that *if* Life has meaning, this must be sought in what, being "beyond" Life, is at once mysterious and measure-giving. Life's meaning is to be found, if at all, neither in some ingredient of Life, nor in Life-as-a-whole, nor in anything outside Life that we could hope to articulate and describe.

I close with some remarks on the implications of this position for the conception of meaning as appropriateness to Life that guided my discussions until this final chapter. It does not imply any departure from the the idea of meaning as appropriateness *tout court*. Indeed, to speak of Life as meaningful in virtue of "responding" to what is mysterious, of "measuring up" to it and of obeying "directives" that it "assigns", is to talk the language of appropriateness. Life can be meaningful, because appropriate to mystery, in the same broad sense that an action can be meaningful as an appropriate response to an order. In what respects, exactly, Life might be thus appropriate is, of course, another matter. But the traditions I mentioned two paragraphs earlier are not without their attempts at least to gesture at these respects. Maybe a person's life, like water, "comes close to the Way" – is appropriate to it – through "benefitting [things] without contending with them", for the Way, as the principle of everything, confronts nothing with which it must contend (Lao Tzu 1985: Ch. 8). Maybe it is this non-contending beneficence that would give human Life significance and worth.

What has to go, it seems, when it comes to the meaning of Life, is the idea of meaning as appropriateness to *Life*. If what is mysterious is both the source of Life's meaning and "beyond Life", then what Life is appropriate to is not itself. I doubt, however, that I would lose sleep over this counter-example to the general formula of meaning as appropriateness to Life. Clearly the question "What does it mean?" becomes a very special question – a "one-off" – when "it" happens to refer to Life itself. One might, therefore, serenely concede that, when it comes to Life, the general formula does not apply. This failure of application can be contained: it need not infect the general strategy.

Still, I end by making a remark that might serve to mitigate the extent of the departure, when it comes to Life's meaning, from the general formula. I have been speaking of the mysterious source of Life's meaning as something "beyond" Life. But that term may not be a happy one: at any rate, it might encourage a picture to which one should not feel committed. This is the picture of mystery as something transcendent – as, say, the cause of Life, or in some other way logically independent of Life. Now that is not at all the way in which the mysterious is envisioned by the traditions and thinkers, friendly to the idea of mystery, referred to above. Some Buddhists, for example, speak of Emptiness not as a transcendent cause of the world, but as something (not some *thing*) of which the world or Life is, as it were, an epiphany. Heidegger reiterates that Being is not disjoint from the beings which it is nevertheless "gives". In particular, without human beings there would be no Being – the point of his metaphors, in his *Letter on Humanism* (1993), of human language as "the house of Being" and of man as "the shepherd of Being".

It is impossible, in the present context, to pursue these heady speculations. Their purpose has simply been to wean one away from the conviction that what is "beyond Life" must – like the theists' God – be visualized as standing outside or before Life. I, for one, find the conceptions gestured at by Buddhist talk of Emptiness and Heideggerian talk of Being "presencing" as Life more attractive than transcendent conceptions. The present point is not to persuade you to feel the same attraction, but to recognize that it is one towards a conception of the relation between Life and mystery on which those two terms are not flatly disjoined. Life, in being appropriate to mystery, is not appropriate to something separate that might have plodded its own ineffable way in the absence of Life. If sense can be made of this conception, that is important. That it would also mitigate the departure from my general formula of meaning as appropriateness to Life is only an extra bonus.

References

Baier, K. 1987. "The Purpose of Man's Existence". In *Life and Meaning: A Reader*, O. Hanfling (ed.), 9–19. Oxford: Blackwell.

Baker, G. P. & P. M. S. Hacker 1980. *Wittgenstein: Meaning and Understanding*. Oxford: Blackwell.

Barthes, R. 1968. *Elements of Semiology*, A. Lavers & C. Smith (trans.). New York: Hill & Wang.

Barthes, R. 1977. *Image, Music, Text*, S. Heath (trans.). New York: Hill & Wang.

Beardsley, M. & W. Wimsatt 1976. "The Intentional Fallacy". In *On Literary Intentions*, D. de Moline (ed.), 1–13. Edinburgh: Edinburgh University Press.

Bell, C. 1920. *Art*. London: Chatto.

Blair, P. Hunter 1996. *Northumberland in the Days of Bede*. Felinfach: Llanerch.

Blixen, K. 1982. *Out of Africa*. Harmondsworth: Penguin.

Borges, J. L. 1979. *The Book of Sand*, N. di Giovanni (trans.). Harmondsworth: Penguin.

Brandom, R. B. 1994. *Making It Explicit*. Cambridge, MA: Harvard University Press.

Brandom, R. B. 2000. *Articulating Reasons: An Introduction to Inferentialism*. Cambridge, MA: Harvard University Press.

Cage, J. 1968. *Silence*. London: Calder & Boyers.

Cassirer, E. 1996. *The Philosophy of Symbolic Forms*, vol. 4, J. Krois (trans.). New Haven, CT: Yale University Press.

Cavell, S. 1996. "Declining Decline: Wittgenstein as a Philosopher of Culture". In *The Cavell Reader*, S. Mulhall (ed.). Oxford: Blackwell.

Chomsky, N. 1968. *Language and Mind*. New York: Harcourt, Brace & World.

Cooper, D. E. 1986. *Metaphor*. Oxford: Blackwell.

Cooper, D. E. 1997. "Communication, Interpretation and System". In *Interfaces: Essays in Honour of Peter Serracino Inglott*, J. Friggieri & S. Busuttil (eds), 3–18. Malta: University of Malta Press.

Cooper, D. E. 2002. *The Measure of Things: Humanism, Humility, and Mystery*. Oxford: Oxford University Press.

Crane, T. 1995. "Meaning". In *The Oxford Companion to Philosophy*, T. Honderich (ed.), 541–2. Oxford: Oxford University Press.

Culler, J. 1983. *On Deconstruction*. London: Routledge & Kegan Paul.

Darwin, C. 1873. *The Expression of Emotion in Animals*. New York: Appleton.

Davidson, D. 1984. *Inquiries into Truth and Interpretation*. Oxford: Clarendon Press.

Davidson, D. 1986a. "A Coherence Theory of Truth and Knowledge". See Lepore (1986), 307–19.

Davidson, D. 1986b. "A Nice Derangement of Epitaphs". See Lepore (1986), 433–46.

Derrida, J. 1976. *Of Grammatology*, G. Spivak (trans.). Baltimore, MD: Johns Hopkins University Press.

Derrida, J. 1981. *Positions*, A. Bass (trans.). Chicago, IL: University of Chicago Press.

Derrida, J. 1982. *Margins of Philosophy*, A. Bass (trans.). Chicago, IL: University of Chicago Press.

Derrida, J. 1988. *Limited Inc.*, S. Weber (trans.). Evanston, IL: Northwestern University Press.

Dilthey, W. 1923–. *Gesammelte Schriften* [19 vols]. Leipzig: Teuber.

Dilthey, W. 1979. *Selected Writings*, H. Rickman (trans.). Cambridge: Cambridge University Press.

Dummett, M. 1976. "What is a Theory of Meaning? (II)". See Evans & McDowell (1976), 67–137.

Evans, G. & J. McDowell (eds) 1976. *Truth and Meaning: Essays in Semantics*. Oxford: Clarendon Press.

Feyerabend, P. 2000. *Conquest of Abundance: A Tale of Abstraction versus the Richness of Being*. Chicago, IL: University of Chicago Press.

Fodor, J. 2001. "Dicing with Shadows", *Times Literary Supplement*, 6 July: 6–8.

Francis, M. & R. Hester 1990. *The Meaning of Gardens*. Cambridge, MA: MIT Press.

Frege, G. 1959. *The Foundations of Arithmetic*, J. L. Austin (trans.). Oxford: Blackwell.

Frege, G. 1966. *The Philosophical Writings of Gottlob Frege*, P. Geach & M. Black (trans.). Oxford: Blackwell.

Frege, G. 1967. *The Basic Laws of Arithmetic: Exposition of the System*, M. Furth (trans.). Berkeley, CA: University of California Press.

Friggieri, J. 1991. *Actions and Speech Actions*. Malta: Minerva.

Gadamer, H.-G. 1977. *Philosophical Hermeneutics*, D. Linge (trans.). Berkeley, CA: University of California Press.

Gao Xingjian 2001. *Soul Mountain*, M. Lee (trans.). London: Flamingo.

Ghosh, A. 2000. *The Glass Palace*. London: HarperCollins.

Goehr, L. 1993. "'Music has no Meaning to Speak of': On the Politics of Musical Interpretation". See Krausz (1993), 177–202.

Grice, H. P. 1989. *Studies in the Ways of Words*. Cambridge, MA: Harvard University Press.

Habermas, J. 1980. "The Hermeneutic Claim to Universality". In *Contemporary Hermeneutics*, J. Bleicher (ed.), 181–212. London: Routledge & Kegan Paul.

Hacking, I. 1975. *What Does Language Matter to Philosophy?* Cambridge: Cambridge University Press.

Hacking, I. 1982. "Language, Truth, and Reason". In *Rationality and Relativism*, M. Hollis & S. Lukes (eds), 48–66. Oxford: Blackwell.

Hahn, R. A. 1973. "Understanding Beliefs", *Current Anthropology* 14.

Hale, B. 1997. "Rule-following, Objectivity and Meaning". See Hale & Wright (1997), 369–96.

Hale, B. & C. Wright (eds) 1997. *A Companion to the Philosophy of Language*. Oxford: Blackwell.

Hanfling, O. (ed.) 1987. *Life and Meaning: A Reader*. Oxford: Blackwell.

Harris, R. 2002. "Looking In for the Meaning Without", *Times Higher Education Supplement*, Feb.: 15.

Harrison, C. & P. Wood (eds) 1992. *Art in Theory: 1900–1990*. Oxford: Blackwell.

Heal, J. 1989. *Fact and Meaning: Quine and Wittgenstein on Philosophy of Language*. Oxford: Blackwell.

Heidegger, M. 1980. *Being and Time*, J. Macquarrie & E. Robinson (trans.). Oxford: Blackwell.

Heidegger, M. 1993. *Basic Writings*, D. F. Krell (ed.). Oxford: Blackwell.

Hepburn, R. 2001. *The Reach of the Aesthetic: Collected Essays on Art and Nature*. Aldershot: Ashgate.

Hirsch, E. D. 1967. *Validity in Interpretation*. New Haven, CT: Yale University Press.

Horwich, P. 1999. *Meaning*. Oxford: Clarendon Press.

Hume, D. 1977. *An Enquiry Concerning Human Understanding*. Indianapolis, IN: Hackett.

Husserl, E. 1970. *Crisis of European Sciences and Transcendental Phenomenology*, D. Carr (trans.). Evanston, IL: Northwestern University Press.

Kant, I. 1951. *The Critique of Judgement*, J. Bernard (trans.). New York: Hafner.

Kerckhoff, A. C. 1964. "Meaning". In *A Dictionary of the Social Sciences*, J. Gould & W. Kolb (eds), 418–20. London: Tavistock.

Kermani, N. 2002. "A Dynamite of the Spirit", *Times Literary Supplement*, March 29: 13–15.

Krausz, M. (ed.) 1993. *The Interpretation of Music: Philosophical Essays*. Oxford: Clarendon Press.

Kripke, S. 1982. *Wittgenstein on Rules and Private Language*. Oxford: Blackwell.

Kundera, M. 1984. *The Unbearable Lightness of Being*, M. Heim (trans.). London: Faber & Faber.

Lakoff, G. & M. Johnson 1980. *Metaphors We Live By*. Chicago, IL: University of Chicago Press.

Lao Tzu 1985. *Tao Te Ching*, D. Lau (trans.). Harmondsworth: Penguin.

Lawrence, T. E. 1969. *Seven Pillars of Wisdom*. Harmondsworth: Penguin.

Leach, E. 1976. *Culture and Communication: The Logic by which Symbols are Connected*. Cambridge: Cambridge University Press.

Lehrer, K. & A. Lehrer (eds) 1970. *Theory of Meaning*. Englewood Cliffs, NJ: Prentice-Hall.

Lepore, E. (ed.) 1986. *Truth and Interpretation: Perspectives on the Philosophy of Donald Davidson*. Oxford: Blackwell.

Lévi-Strauss, C. 1966. "Overture to *Le cru et le cuit*". In *Structuralism*, Yale French Studies. New Haven, CT: Yale University Press.

Lewis, D. 1969. *Convention: A Philosophical Study*. Cambridge, MA: Harvard University Press.

Loar, B. 1995. "Meaning" In *The Cambridge Dictionary of Philosophy*, R. Audi (ed.), 471–6. Cambridge: Cambridge University Press.

Locke, J. 1975. *An Essay Concerning Human Understanding*. Oxford: Clarendon Press.

Luntley, M. 1991. "The Transcendental Grounds of Meaning and the Place of Silence". In *Meaning Scepticism*, K. Puhl (ed.), 170–88. Berlin: de Gruyter.

Lyas, C. 1997. *Aesthetics*. London: UCL Press.

Lycan, W. G. 2000. *Philosophy of Language: A Contemporary Introduction*. London: Routledge.

Lyotard, J.-F. 1986. *The Postmodern Condition: A Report on Knowledge*, G. Bennington & B. Massumi (trans.). Manchester: Manchester University Press.

McDowell, J. 1976. "Truth-conditions, Bivalence and Verificationism". See Evans & McDowell (1976), 42–66.

McDowell, J. 1984. "Wittgenstein on Following a Rule", *Synthese* 58: 325–63.

MacIntyre, A. 1973. "The Idea of a Social Science". In *The Philosophy of Social Action*, A. Ryan (ed.), 15–32. Oxford: Oxford University Press.

MacIntyre, A. 1992. "Colors, Cultures, and Practices", *Midwest Studies in Philosophy* XVII.

Marcel, G. 1948. *The Philosophy of Existence*, M. Harari (trans.). London: Harvill.

Marcel, G. 1949. *Being and Having*, K. Farrar (trans.). London: Dacre.

Merleau-Ponty, M. 1962. *Phenomenology of Perception*, C. Smith (trans.). London: Routledge & Kegan Paul.

Merleau-Ponty, M. 1964. *Sense and Non-Sense*, H. L. & P. A. Dreyfus (trans.). Evanston, IL: Northwestern University Press.

Mulhall, S. 2001. *Inheritance and Originality: Wittgenstein, Heidegger, Kierkegaard*. Oxford: Clarendon Press.

Nietzsche, F. 1954. "Twilight of the Idols". In *The Portable Nietzsche*, W. Kaufmann (trans.). New York: Viking.

Nozick, R. 1981. *Philosophical Explanations*. Oxford: Clarendon Press.

Ogden, C. K. & I. A. Richards 1923. *The Meaning of Meaning*. New York: Harcourt, Brace and World.

Ondaatje, M. 2000. *Anil's Ghost*. London: Picador.

Panofsky, E. 1970. *Meaning in the Visual Arts*. Harmondsworth: Penguin.

Pareto, V. 1935. *The Mind and Society*. New York: Harcourt Brace.

Perec, G. 1988. *Life: A User's Manual*. London: Collins Harvill.

Putnam, H. 1975. *Mind, Language and Reality: Philosophical Papers*, Vol. 2. Cambridge: Cambridge University Press.

Quine, W. V. 1960. *Word and Object*. Cambridge, MA: MIT Press.

Quine, W. V. 1970. "Philosophical Progress in Language Theory", *Metaphilosophy* 1: 1–8.

Quine, W. V. 1996. "Meaning". In *The Philosophy of Language*, A. Martinich (ed.), 446–55. Oxford: Oxford University Press.

Rescher, N. 1980. "Conceptual Schemes", *Midwest Studies in Philosophy* V: 323–46.

Ricoeur, P. 1977. *The Rule of Metaphor*, R. Czerny (trans.). Toronto: University of Toronto Press.

Roy, A. 1998. *The God of Small Things*. London: Flamingo.

Rundle, B. 1979. *Grammar in Philosophy*. Oxford: Clarendon Press.

Ruskin, J. 1903–12. *Sesame and Lilies*, in his *Collected Works*, vol. XVIII. London: Allen.

Sartre, J.-P. 1957. *Being and Nothingness*, H. Barnes (trans.). London: Methuen.

Saussure, F. 1966. *Course in General Linguistics*, W. Baskin (trans.). New York: McGraw-Hill.

Schelling, F. W. J. 1978. *System of Transcendental Idealism*, P. Heath (trans.). Charlottesville, VA: University of Virginia Press.

Schwandt, T. A. 2000. "Three Epistemological Stances for Qualitative Inquiry". In *Handbook of Qualitative Research*, N. Denzin & Y. Lincoln (eds), 189–213. London: Sage.

Scruton, R. 1993. "Notes on the Meaning of Music". See Krausz (1993), 193–202.

Searle, J. R. 1979. *Expression and Meaning*. New York: Cambridge University Press.

Searle, J. R. 1983. *Intentionality: An Essay in the Philosophy of Mind*. Cambridge: Cambridge University Press.

Seferis, G. 1982. *On the Greek Style*, R. Warner (trans.). Limni: Harvey.

Serracino Inglott, P. 1995. *Peopled Silence*. Malta: University of Malta Press.

Sharpe, R. A. 2000. *Music and Humanism: An Essay in the Aesthetics of Music*. Oxford: Oxford University Press.

Sperber, D. 1975a. "Rudiments de rhétorique cognitive", *Poétique* 23.

Sperber, D. 1975b. *Rethinking Symbolism*, A. Morton (trans.). Cambridge: Cambridge University Press.

Sperber, D. & D. Wilson 1986. *Relevance: Communication and Cognition*. Oxford: Blackwell.

Spinosa, C. 1992. "Derrida and Heidegger: Iterability and *Ereignis*". In *Heidegger: a Critical Reader*, H. Dreyfus & H. Hall (eds), 270–97. Oxford: Blackwell.

Steiner, G. 1989. *Real Presences*. London: Faber & Faber.

Strawson, P. 1996. "Meaning and Truth". In *The Philosophy of Language*, 3rd edn, A. P. Martinich (ed.). Oxford: Oxford University Press.

Stroud, B. 1996. "Mind, Meaning and Practice". In *The Cambridge Compan-*

ion to Wittgenstein, H. Sluga & D. Stern (eds), 296–319. Cambridge: Cambridge University Press.

Tarski, A. 1956. *Logic, Semantics, Metamathematics*, J. Woodger (trans.). Oxford: Clarendon Press.

Taylor, C. 1985. *Human Agency and Language: Philosophical Papers I*. Cambridge: Cambridge University Press.

Travis, C. 1994. "On Constraints of Generality", *Proceedings of the Aristotelian Society* **94**: 165–88.

Travis, C. 1997. "Pragmatics". See Hale & Wright (1997), 87–107.

Weber, M. 1922. *Wirtschaft und Gesellschaft*. Tübingen: Mohr.

Wheeler, S. C. 1986. "Indeterminacy of French Interpretation". See Lepore (1986), 477–94.

Winch, P. 1963. *The Idea of a Social Science*. London: Routledge & Kegan Paul.

Wittgenstein, L. 1960. *The Blue and Brown Books*. Oxford: Blackwell.

Wittgenstein, L. 1969. *Philosophical Investigations*, G. Anscombe (trans.). Oxford: Blackwell.

Wittgenstein, L. 1975. *Zettel*, G. Anscombe (trans.). Oxford: Blackwell.

Wittgenstein, L. 1980. *Culture and Value*, P. Winch (trans.). Oxford: Blackwell.

Wittgenstein, L. 1988. *Tractatus Logico-Philosophicus*, D. Pears & B. McGuiness (trans.). London: Routledge.

Wright, C. 1980. *Wittgenstein and the Foundations of Mathematics*. London: Duckworth.

Wright, C. 1984. "Kripke's Account of the Argument against Private Language", *Journal of Philosophy* **81**, 759–78.

Young, J. 2001. *Heidegger's Philosophy of Art*. Oxford: Clarendon Press.

Zhuang Zi 1984. *Wisdom of the Daoist Masters: The Works of Lao Zi, Lie Zi, and Zhuang Zi*, L. Wieger (trans.). Lampeter: Llanerch.

Index